W9-ACJ-513

—Diseases and People—

POLIO

Alvin and Virginia Silverstein and
Laura Silverstein Nunn

Enslow Publishers, Inc.

40 Industrial Road   PO Box 38
Box 398   Aldershot
Berkeley Heights, NJ 07922   Hants GU12 6BP
USA   UK
http://www.enslow.com

CODMAN SQUARE

SEP - - 2001

Acknowledgments

The authors would like to thank Maggie Yax, the Albert B. Sabin archivist at the Hauck Center of the Cincinnati Medical Heritage Center, for her careful reading of the manuscript and her helpful suggestions.

Many thanks, too, to John and Maggie Prestwich, who generously shared the fascinating details of their life after polio. Their warm hearts and indomitable spirits have touched and inspired us.

Copyright © 2001 by Alvin and Virginia Silverstein and Laura Silverstein Nunn

All rights reserved.

No part of this book may be reproduced by any means
without the written permission of the publisher.

Library of Congress Cataloging-in-Publication Data

Silverstein, Alvin.
Polio / Alvin and Virginia Silverstein and Laura Silverstein Nunn.
p. cm. — (Diseases and people)
ISBN 0-7660-1592-0
1. Poliomyelitis—Juvenile literature. [1. Poliomyelitis. 2. Diseases.] I. Silverstein,
Virginia B. II. Nunn, Laura Silverstein. III. Title. IV. Series.
RC180.1 .S57   2001
616.8'35—dc21   00-010993

Printed in the United States of America

10 9 8 7 6 5 4 3 2 1

To Our Readers:
We have done our best to make sure all Internet addresses in this book were active and appropriate when we went to press. However, the author and the publisher have no control over and assume no liability for the material available on those Internet sites or on other Web sites they may link to. Any comments or suggestions can be sent by e-mail to comments@enslow.com or to the address on the back cover.

Illustration Credits: Centers for Disease Control, p. 93; Centers for Disease Control, Barbara Rice, p. 94; John Russo, p. 100; Julia Morris, p. 89 (bottom); Karen Bornemann Spies, p. 81; LifeART image copyright 1998 Lippincott Williams & Wilkins, all rights reserved, p. 29; Maggie Prestwich, p. 67; The March of Dimes, pp. 6, 8, 25, 33, 74; Mattel Corporation, p. 87; Mike Roberts, p. 89 (top); Minnesota Historical Society, p. 62; National Library of Medicine, pp. 23, 38, 46, 49, 54; National Library of Medicine, Hal Rumel, p. 55; National Library of Medicine, Louis Schmidt, p. 41; WHO EPI Information System, p. 75; World Health Organization, pp. 15, 77; World Health Organization, Marcel Crozet, p. 96.

Cover Illustration: World Health Organization, Marcel Crozet.

The cover image shows a young girl receiving a dose of the oral polio vaccine.

Contents

CD BR
J
RC180.1
.S57
2001

POLIO

What is it? A highly contagious disease caused by a virus.

Who gets it? Mainly children, but people of any age who are not immune to the poliovirus can catch it. The illness is much more severe in teenagers and adults. Currently it occurs naturally only in a few parts of the world, such as India and Africa.

How do you get it? Usually the virus is transmitted by mouth, after contact with infected people or their feces, or after eating or drinking food or water contaminated with the virus. A small number of cases are caused by taking the live type of polio vaccine.

What are the symptoms? A slight fever, headache, sore throat, stomach pain, and vomiting develop about seven to fourteen days after exposure to the virus. These symptoms last for one to three days. If the virus invades the central nervous system, more serious symptoms may develop: a higher fever, headache, stiff neck, vomiting, fatigue, back pain, pain or stiffness in the neck, leg pain, and muscle weakness or spasms. In about one percent of cases, paralysis (loss of movement) of the limbs and/or breathing muscles develops. Symptoms may also include sensitivity to touch, difficulty swallowing, muscle pain, irritability, constipation, or difficulties in urinating.

How is it treated? Paralysis is treated with heat packs applied to the muscles and muscle-stretching exercises. A machine to help the patient breathe, such as an iron lung or respirator, may be needed if the breathing muscles are paralyzed.

How can it be prevented? Today, polio is almost nonexistent, thanks to the polio vaccine. Children receive three doses of polio vaccine in the first two years of life and a booster dose when they start school. The United States Centers for Disease Control and Prevention (CDC) currently recommends the use of injectable vaccine made from inactivated virus.

This poster, an advertisement encouraging people to give money to the March of Dimes, features Donald Anderson, the "poster child" for 1946.

1

A Devastating Disease

Franklin Delano Roosevelt was a strong, powerful man, who served for more than twelve years as president of the United States (1933-1945). He was admired for his determination and leadership as he steered the American people out of the Great Depression and toward victory in World War II. Yet at the same time, Roosevelt was fighting his own personal battle against the effects of a devastating disease—polio.

Roosevelt's private struggle began when he was thirty-nine, in the summer of 1921. After an exhausting election campaign in 1920, when he ran for the office of vice-president of the United States and lost, Roosevelt was vacationing with his family at his summer home on Campobello Island, off the coast of New Brunswick, Canada. Roosevelt had been feeling a little run-down when he arrived on the island. But that did not stop him from hiking and swimming with his family.

On August 10, 1921, Roosevelt was out sailing with his wife and children when they spotted a forest fire on a nearby island.

They spent several hours putting out the fire. Feeling exhausted, Roosevelt took a swim in the icy waters of the Bay of Fundy to refresh himself. When he came back to the house, he was too tired to change out of his wet clothes and sat for awhile reading his mail and a few newspapers. Roosevelt had chills that lasted much of the night. He thought he was just fighting a bad cold.

The next morning, Roosevelt noticed that the muscles in his right knee were weak. By the afternoon, his right leg was too weak to support his weight. That night, the left knee also became weak, and by the next morning he could no longer stand up or walk. His temperature had risen to 102 degrees, and he had pain in his back. Soon his back, arms, and hands became partially paralyzed, or unable to move.

Roosevelt was afraid that he might have polio, but neither the local family doctor nor a prominent surgeon, who was vacationing nearby, agreed with that diagnosis when they saw Roosevelt. Finally, Roosevelt's family contacted Dr. Samuel Levine at the Harvard Infantile Paralysis Commission. Dr. Levine called Dr. Robert Lovett, a medical specialist at Harvard, who arrived at Campobello to examine Roosevelt. Dr. Lovett diagnosed infantile paralysis, the name that was used for polio at that time.

Roosevelt was determined to walk again. Over the next seven years, he dedicated his life to regaining his strength. By exercising regularly, Roosevelt was able to strengthen his arm and shoulder muscles. Frequent massages were also helpful in his treatment. Roosevelt also tried bathing and swimming in a warm pool at Warm Springs, a thermal spa in Georgia. These treatments helped soothe his weakened legs. In fact, he was so convinced that the heated pools benefited his condition that he later bought the Warm Springs property and made it available to other polio survivors for their rehabilitation.[1]

Roosevelt's condition did improve a little, but he was never able to walk again. That did not stop him from leading an active life, however. He became active in politics again, and in November 1932 he was elected president of the United States. During election campaigns and throughout his four terms in office, Roosevelt downplayed his disability. Although he spent most of the time in a wheelchair at home, he wore hip-high leg braces (metal supports) and held onto a cane or someone's arm when he needed to stand for public appearances.[2]

Although Roosevelt took care to avoid being photographed in a wheelchair or in other situations that would contradict the strong, independent image he presented to the public, Roosevelt spent a lot of time, energy, and his own money in the fight against polio. In addition to the Warm Springs resort, in 1938 he helped to found the National Foundation for Infantile Paralysis (NFIP), and actively promoted its work in helping others with polio and seeking a cure for this devastating disease. This organization sponsored the March of Dimes, a charitable campaign that asked people to send in dimes for polio research.[3] Eventually, the NFIP itself became known as the March of Dimes Foundation, and its fund-raising campaigns led to the development of the polio vaccines that are used today.

Franklin D. Roosevelt is the most famous person with polio in our history. During his time, polio was a greatly feared disease that affected thousands of people each year. It was originally called infantile paralysis because it often occurred in babies and children, and the disease sometimes resulted in paralysis. It was generally associated with lower-class families and poor living conditions. But Roosevelt was a grown man who came from an affluent background, and even he was not safe from polio, proving this popular perception to be inaccurate.

President Franklin Delano Roosevelt (left) counts dimes with Basil O'Connor at the White House in 1938. FDR was one of the founders of the National Foundation for Infantile Paralysis (NFIP), an organization that later became the March of Dimes Foundation.

Polio is a highly contagious disease that is caused by a virus (a microorganism that could pass through filters small enough to trap the smallest bacteria). The poliovirus attacks nerve cells in the brain and spinal cord, which control the muscles of the body. A wide range of symptoms can result, and each case is different. A polio infection can range from a mild illness to partial or complete paralysis. When key nerve cells are damaged, they can no longer send signals to the muscles they control. Without receiving messages from the nerve cells, these muscles can no longer contract and move body parts. In some cases, the muscles that work in breathing are affected, and the person cannot breathe without a mechanical aid, such as an iron lung. This cumbersome and frightening metal apparatus was what people thought of first whenever polio was mentioned. The virus can also affect the muscles that move the limbs. If the nerve cells that are damaged by the poliovirus are able to recover from the injury, then the muscles will gradually regain their function. But if the nerve cells are destroyed by the virus, the paralysis will be permanent, and the muscles will atrophy, or wither.

There are no drugs that can kill the poliovirus or stop it from causing damage once it has invaded the body. Medical workers can only treat the symptoms of this disease to make the patients feel more comfortable and to try to prevent further damage. Heat packs, massage, and stretching can help keep the muscles healthy while the body gradually regains whatever nerve function it can.

Although there is no cure for polio, we are on the threshold of seeing it disappear from the world forever because there are effective means of preventing it. Vaccines developed in the 1950s can protect people from becoming infected by the poliovirus. In fact, these vaccines have been used so widely and have worked so well that in the developed countries today, the only polio cases that occur are those caused by the vaccine itself. Soon even vaccine-induced cases should no longer be a problem, however. Public health authorities have recommended switching to a safer type of vaccine, which cannot cause an active polio infection.

World health agencies are aiming to eradicate polio throughout the world by the early 2000s through an active vaccination campaign in the few areas where it is still common. Then polio immunizations may no longer be needed.

2

What Is Polio?

In the summer of 1958, six-year-old Mark Sauer spent the weekends with his family at a park near their home in Detroit, Michigan. They often had picnics and played in the water. Near the end of the summer around Labor Day, Mark got up to get ready to go home and suddenly felt dizzy and confused. He did not say anything to his parents, but he felt worse on the car ride home. That night Mark and his family went to the movies, and the boy developed a fever and began to sweat. His parents thought he had the flu, but he was still so ill the next morning that they took him to the hospital. Considering the symptoms and the fact that there had been a major polio epidemic in the area that summer, the doctor suspected polio. Mark's parents were horrified at the very word.

Mark was admitted to the hospital and was given a test called a spinal tap, in which fluid from the channel around the spinal cord is examined for signs of infection. This test would confirm that he had polio. He was brought into an isolation ward to keep him from spreading the disease to other hospital patients. His fever had climbed to 107 degrees and remained there for several days. Then Mark also developed spinal meningitis—an inflammation of the membranes covering the brain and spinal cord, not an uncommon condition in polio patients. His neck started to curve up into a stiff horseshoe shape. Finally, after about five days, his fever went down, and his neck returned to normal.

By that time, however, Mark's ankles, lower legs, and one hip were weakened, making it very difficult to walk. At age six, Mark had to learn how to walk all over again, one step at a time. During months of physical therapy, he worked on exercises to strengthen his ankles, knees, and lower legs. The doctors also suggested that Mark should get into sports activities as soon as he was strong enough. Mark was determined to get better. Eventually, he was able to run. He even made the school's ice hockey team. These athletic activities helped to keep Mark's muscles strong, and he grew up without any lingering effects of the disease.[1]

In September 1953, thirteen-year-old Charlene Pugleasa invited friends to her house for a big slumber party. About a week later, Charlene started to feel sick. During a car ride, her brother jokingly poked at her ribs, and she started screaming because it hurt so much when he touched her. That night, she went to the movies with some friends. In Sudan, Minnesota, where Charlene lived, there was only one movie theater in the area. She and her friends usually walked the two miles it took to get there. At the theater, Charlene felt really sick—she had a sore throat, a headache, her body hurt with a shooting pain, and she had a terrible backache. As they walked home from the theater, Charlene became exhausted, and her legs became weak. That night, after she finally got home, she got even sicker.

The next couple of days were really rough. Charlene had chills, and her fever was really high. At one point, she could not even walk up the stairs; her legs were too weak to carry her, and her back was very painful. Charlene went to the hospital that night. The doctor thought it could be a kidney infection, so he took a urine sample, then sent Charlene home. The next day, Charlene's fever had gone up to 104 degrees, and she was still in terrible pain. Her mother called the doctor and insisted he come over right away. When the doctor arrived, he said the tests showed Charlene did not have a kidney infection. When he tried to lift Charlene's head, she screamed. Then he lifted her leg, and she felt pain shoot up through her leg and up her back, then up her neck and into her head. The doctor took her mother aside and told her it looked like Charlene had infantile paralysis, also known as polio.

Charlene's parents took her back to the hospital, and she had a spinal tap to confirm the diagnosis. She was then brought into the contagion unit—the area containing infectious, or contagious, patients. There were iron lung machines all around the unit. She could hear the sounds of pumping, hissing, and gushing as they breathed life into the patients.

Every day Charlene tried to move her head and legs. She could not lift her head, and she lifted her legs only with great difficulty. Then one day, she could not move her legs at all—they were paralyzed.

The nurses used hot packs to ease the pain in the muscles. These packs were strips of heavy woolen blankets, soaked in boiling water then wrung out and wrapped all over her body. Charlene also worked with the physical therapist to strengthen her muscles. She went home after about a month, and her father set up a weight-training program to strengthen her muscles even further. At home, Charlene was given hot baths, did stretching exercises with her mother, and worked with the weights. Eventually, Charlene fought her way back and managed to walk again, without the aid of any braces or crutches.[2]

A Viral Disease

The full medical name for polio is poliomyelitis. Poliomyelitis describes an inflammation of the gray matter of the spinal cord; its name was taken from the Greek words *polios* (meaning "gray"), *myelos* ("marrow" or "spinal cord"), and *itis* ("inflammation"). The gray matter of the spinal cord contains anterior horn cells, which are motor neurons (nerve cells) that send messages to control muscles of the legs, arms, trunk, diaphragm, abdomen, and pelvis. If these motor neurons are harmed, and the signals they generate are disrupted, the muscles may not work. Then the parts the muscles control may become paralyzed.

While the poliovirus destroys the major motor neurons in the gray matter of the spinal cord, it does not touch any of the sensory cells of the spinal cord. These sensory cells transmit the incoming messages involving pain, temperature, position, balance, and vibration to the brain. That is why a patient can feel severe pain in a paralyzed arm, leg, or back.[3]

Like many other viruses, the poliovirus consists of a core of RNA (ribonucleic acid, a biochemical that contains all the instructions for infecting hosts and making new viruses) surrounded by proteins and lipids. It "comes alive" and can reproduce only within a living cell. When the poliovirus comes in contact with a suitable host (usually a human, although the poliovirus can infect monkeys in the laboratory), it attaches itself to the outer membrane of a host cell and penetrates inside it. There, like an annoying uninvited guest, the virus takes over. It

Not Quite a Fitting Name

The name *poliomyelitis* was first used in the late 1870s, before scientists knew the disease was caused by a virus. The poliovirus can produce a variety of effects in the body, ranging from a mild childhood disease to paralysis. In many cases, the poliovirus does not even attack the motor neurons. It is only the paralytic form of the disease that the name truly describes.

Nonetheless, the name *polio* is used to identify all conditions caused by any one of the three strains of poliovirus. The three strains are known as type 1, or Brunhilde; type 2, or Lansing; and type 3, or Leon.

uses the host cell's gene-copying machinery to direct the mass production of new virus particles.

The virus's ability to infect body cells depends partly on how virulent, or poisonous, it is. For instance, a highly virulent poliovirus is more likely to cause severe, crippling symptoms in its host; a mildly virulent poliovirus may produce milder symptoms or none at all. The poliovirus is also more likely to take hold when a person's defenses are weakened from an illness, such as AIDS, for instance.

The poliovirus enters its human host through the mouth, after the host has touched a person infected with the disease or swallowed food or water contaminated by the feces of an infected person. The virus then settles in the throat or in the lining of the intestine, where it quickly multiplies. In mild cases, the viruses stop reproducing in a week or two, and the illness is over without any serious health problems. But viruses continue to be shed in the host's feces for several weeks after the infection. During this time the person can transmit the infection to others.

Sometimes the poliovirus travels into the host's bloodstream and may find its way into the central nervous system. Infection of nerve cells in the brain or spinal cord may lead to paralysis. The seriousness of paralysis depends on the amount of damage to the nerve cells. The poliovirus does not always destroy nerve cells completely. The paralyzed muscles may return to normal functioning months later. But nerve cells that are destroyed completely cannot recover, and paralysis may be permanent.

If some of the nerve cells leading to the paralyzed body part are still alive, they can take over the work of those that were destroyed. The affected person may then be able to regain muscle control months later. The healthy nerve cells will sprout new branches, which will grow into the paralyzed body part and make contact with the muscles that move it. These motor neurons can

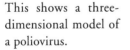

This shows a three-dimensional model of a poliovirus.

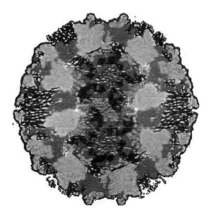

then carry signals from the central nervous system to the muscles and control their movements.

A single motor neuron will take over as many as four to five muscle fibers. That means that a motor neuron that normally works two hundred muscle fibers may now control between eight hundred and one thousand fibers. This kind of nerve replacement is so effective that a muscle that has lost up to half of its nerve fibers can regain its normal strength. The reason it takes months to regain strength is that nerve cell growth is a very slow process. The fastest a nerve can grow is about one millimeter per day. It may take up to a year or more to completely restore the nerve connections to a paralyzed arm or leg.[4]

In some cases, the poliovirus attacks the breathing muscles. This can cause serious trouble. As a result, the patient cannot breathe. Many patients need to be supported by a respirator, such as the iron lung, until their breathing muscles get strong enough to work on their own. As many as 50 percent of these victims die.

The Body Defends Itself

The first cells that are attacked by a virus are unable to defend themselves. But several hours before an infected cell produces and releases copies of the virus, a protein called interferon is released into the fluids surrounding the cell. This chemical sends a message to neighboring cells to make an antiviral protein that will fight off viruses. Then, when the virus tries to attack neighboring cells that have produced the antiviral protein, they are able to disobey the virus's orders. Interferon helps delay the spread of infection until the body's other defenses can get to the scene.

An hour or so after a virus invasion, cells in the lining of the digestive system also give off various chemicals that cause inflammation: swelling, pain, heat, and redness around the area of infection. These changes help to slow down virus reproduction, while also making it easier for white blood cells, the body's roving disease fighters, to move around. The white cells can leave the bloodstream and swim through the fluids in the gaps between body cells.

The chemicals released by virus-damaged cells act as distress signals, calling in several kinds of white blood cells. Some white cells gobble down invading germs, destroying them before they can infect cells. Others are able to recognize foreign chemicals, such as the proteins on the outer coat of a virus. Some white blood cells produce antibodies, proteins that contain mirror images of portions of the surface of virus proteins. Antibodies attach to viruses, preventing them from attacking their target cells and making it easier for body defenders to destroy them.

Once a person has produced antibodies that protect against a particular virus, his or her body will be able to prevent future infections by that virus. In other words, the person has become immune to that disease. Some of these specific antibodies continue to circulate in the blood for years, ready to leap into action should the same type of virus attack again.

However, it is important to point out that a person who develops a polio infection has a lifelong immunity to only the one particular strain of poliovirus that caused it. Since there are three types of polioviruses, immunity to all strains of polioviruses occurs only after being infected by each of them or after receiving a vaccine that stimulates protection against the three different strains.

It generally takes about two weeks to make an adequate supply of antibodies to fight a virus the body has never met before; during that time the viruses multiply while the body's less specific defenses try to keep them in check. How fast and how well the body's defenders work determines whether the virus will be wiped out or survive to spread and damage the body.

Who Gets Polio?

Polio is often considered a childhood disease because it is more common in infants and young children. But it can affect anyone who has not been vaccinated, including older children, teens, and adults. In older individuals the effects of polio are much more serious: many patients are crippled and killed. By the 1950s, polio cases in the United States occurred mainly in children five to nine years old. However, two thirds of those patients who died were over fifteen.[5]

Certain factors may make people more vulnerable to polio. Exhaustion is one factor. A person who is worn out from over-exertion or excessive activity may develop a weakened immune system. For example, Franklin D. Roosevelt's defenses may have been worn down after he fought a fire, then stayed in his wet clothes after taking a swim in chilly waters. When the body's defenses are weakened, the poliovirus can do more damage than if the body is healthy and strong. Polio can also be dangerous to immunocompromised patients—people who have impaired immune systems due to illnesses such as AIDS or leukemia.

In the United States, polio immunizations through the use of vaccines have protected against all naturally-occurring polio cases. (About eight to ten cases of paralytic polio caused by the oral vaccine occur in the United States each year.) Polio still occurs in other parts of the world, such as parts of Africa, India, and Pakistan. In 1999, just over seven thousand polio cases were reported.[6]

Danger from a Common Operation

Years ago, when people complained of frequent severe sore throats, doctors often performed a tonsillectomy (the surgical removal of the tonsils). Up to the 1970s, tonsillectomy operations were fairly common. Doctors believed that if a person's tonsils were removed, these swollen lumps of tissue would no longer cause a problem. (These days, doctors realize the importance of tonsils—they contain white blood cells, which help to fight infection; so tonsillectomies are now less common.) During polio epidemics, the common tonsillectomy procedure turned dangerous for some people.

This fact was demonstrated in the early 1940s in a family whose five children all had their tonsils taken out on the same day. All of these children later developed a severe form of polio, which affected the central nervous system, eventually causing swallowing and breathing problems. One child died. It was believed that these children had probably been harboring the poliovirus in their throats. The poliovirus then traveled along exposed nerve endings during surgery, to the central nervous system, where it caused serious damage.[7]

Spreading Polio

Polio can be spread when someone comes into contact with throat secretions of infected people. Sneezing or coughing may spray out virus particles onto nearby objects or people. By touching a contaminated object, a person can pick up the virus particles and later transfer them to his or her mouth by an unwary touch. After entering the mouth, virus particles can multiply in the throat.

Polio is so contagious that authorities used to close swimming pools and movie theaters during the summertime in epidemic areas, hoping to decrease the amount of close contact between potential carriers. Hospital patients were also kept in isolation to avoid spreading the disease to other patients or visitors. Unfortunately, people who have very mild polio symptoms may not even know it. They may then unknowingly spread the infection to others.

Polio can also be spread when people swallow food or water that is contaminated with the poliovirus. Virus particles can be found in human feces for weeks after infection and may contaminate swimming pools or city water supplies. Poliovirus from feces can also get on a person's hands when he or she uses the toilet. Therefore, "dirty fingers" may also be involved in spreading the disease, especially among children who spend time playing together.

This transmission route was vividly demonstrated in 1954, when Queen Elizabeth II visited Western Australia during a polio epidemic. Health experts wondered if they should forbid the local children to participate in the community activities during the queen's visit or run the risk of exploding a polio epidemic among the crowds that would gather to see her. Finally, they decided to let children attend the festivities, but urged families and teachers in charge to be sure to wash the children's hands

QUARANTINE

POLIOMYELITIS

All persons are forbidden to enter or leave these premises without the permission of the HEALTH OFFICER under PENALTY OF THE LAW.

This notice is posted in compliance with the SANITARY CODE OF CONNECTICUT and must not be removed without permission of the HEALTH OFFICER.

Form D-1-Po.   Health Officer.

When polio epidemics were common, extreme measures were taken to prevent its spread. But quarantine (isolation of patients) does not help much because polio can also be spread by people with mild cases, who may not realize they are ill.

with soap and water after they went to the bathroom. This precaution worked: During and right after the queen's visit, the number of new polio cases fell dramatically.

Polio outbreaks usually occurred in the summer to early fall. This period became known as polio season. Scientists did not know and still do not know exactly why polio cases exploded during the summer months and went into hibernation in the cold weather months. There were a number of theories. One explanation suggested that polio may have erupted because many people gathered and interacted more often during the warm, summer months, spreading their germs. Or possibly the excessive activity during the summertime made people more tired and therefore more susceptible to the disease. Or maybe the poliovirus itself was more active at warm temperatures.[8]

Polio Symptoms

A person who has been infected with the poliovirus will usually develop symptoms from seven to fourteen days after exposure, although the incubation period may actually range anywhere from five to thirty-five days. Symptoms may be mild or severe, depending on the location of infection and the amount of damage. Children under five are more likely to experience mild symptoms; older children, teenagers, and adults may develop more serious symptoms.

When people hear the word *polio*, they usually think of a crippling disease that devastates its victims. But in reality, about 90 percent of polio infections are actually mild, causing few symptoms or none at all. In these cases, the infection takes place in the throat and intestines, and causes flu-like symptoms: a slight fever, headache, sore throat, stomach pain, or vomiting. These symptoms are usually mild, lasting for about one to three days. People can make a complete recovery with no lingering effects of the disease.

Nonparalytic Polio

In about 5 to 10 percent of polio cases, the symptoms worsen a few days after the mild symptoms. The poliovirus gets into the bloodstream, and then invades the central nervous system, causing meningitis (infection of the membranes covering the brain and spinal cord). And more serious symptoms may develop: a higher fever, headache, stiff neck, vomiting, fatigue,

This early March of Dimes poster shows a young girl in a wheelchair.

back pain, pain or stiffness in the neck, leg pain, and muscle weakness or spasms, but no paralysis is involved. This form of polio is sometimes called nonparalytic poliomyelitis.

Paralytic Polio

Only one percent of polio infections actually develop into what is called paralytic poliomyelitis. However, this small percentage can translate into thousands of actual people, depending on the size of the population. In this type of polio, the poliovirus attacks and damages the motor neurons in the spinal cord that control the muscles. Early symptoms include a high fever, headache, stiff neck and back, muscle weakness, sensitivity to touch, difficulty swallowing, muscle pain, irritability, constipation, or difficulties in urinating.

Symptoms worsen over the next few days after the first signs of the illness. Muscles become so weak that the patient is unable to move the body parts that are affected. Paralysis may develop gradually over the course of several days, or all at once within a few hours. Usually paralysis is complete when the fever breaks. Normally, muscles are used continually for various movements, which keep them strong. When a limb is paralyzed, however, its muscles no longer work. Paralyzed limbs will begin to atrophy (waste away) because of their lack of mobility.

The patient may develop paralysis in just one arm or leg, or in any combination of all four limbs. Even the neck can be affected. When throat muscles are paralyzed, the patient cannot cough, swallow, or even speak. Paralytic polio can be very dangerous when the breathing muscles or chest muscles are paralyzed.[9]

Types of Paralytic Polio

There are three main types of paralytic polio. The name of each condition describes the location and severity of the paralyzed muscles.

Spinal paralytic polio: This is the most common type of paralytic polio, caused by an infection in the spinal cord. It leaves its victims crippled, producing paralysis in the arms and/or legs. Legs are usually affected more often than the arms. Rarely does spinal polio result in death.

Respiratory polio: The poliovirus attacks the respiratory (breathing) or chest muscles, making it difficult or impossible for the patient to breathe without help from a respirator. This condition is very dangerous, and may result in death in as many as 50 percent of its victims.

Bulbar polio: The poliovirus attacks the nerve cells that are found just above the spinal cord in a region called the "bulb," or brain stem. These nerve cells control the pharynx (throat) and larynx (voice box) muscles. When these areas are affected, the patient may have serious problems swallowing, breathing, and speaking. This is a dangerous form of polio. Secretions collect in the throat and may block the airway (trachea), which may cause the patient to suffocate.[10]

How Breathing Works

Before we can understand what happens when the poliovirus attacks a person's breathing apparatus, we need to examine how the breathing process normally works.

The respiratory system looks very much like an upside-down tree. When you breathe, air comes in through the mouth and nose, goes down the pharynx and through the larynx (voice box), and continues down the main breathing tube, called the windpipe or trachea. The air then goes through two large bronchial tubes (bronchi), which lead into the right and left lungs.

The main breathing muscle is the diaphragm. This is a dome-shaped sheet of muscle that separates the chest cavity on top (which holds the heart and lungs) from the abdominal cavity (which holds the stomach and intestines) below. When you inhale, the diaphragm contracts, moving the "floor" of the chest cavity downward; meanwhile, the chest muscles lift the rib cage up and outward. This muscle action makes the chest cavity expand and creates a partial vacuum. Air is drawn in through the nose or mouth and down the passageways into the lungs. When you exhale, the diaphragm and chest muscles relax, raising the floor and making the chest cavity smaller. There is less room for air in the lungs, so the air flows up the airways and out through the nose. All these muscle actions take place automatically without thinking about them, although you can control breathing to some degree, making it deeper or faster, if you make a conscious effort.

When the poliovirus attacks the breathing muscles, the automatic breathing process breaks down. Damage to nerves serving the diaphragm or chest muscles prevents these muscles from contracting. Even with a conscious effort, the person cannot expand the chest cavity, and air does not flow into the lungs. In addition,

Respiratory System

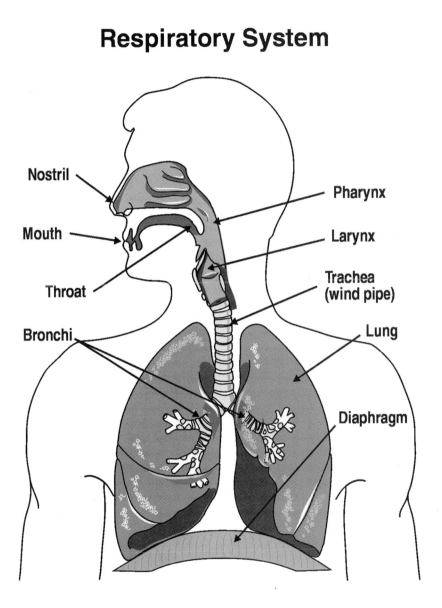

Polio can affect the nerves and muscles of the respiratory system, making breathing difficult or impossible.

damage to the nerves that control the muscles of the throat and windpipe can make swallowing and breathing difficult.

Post-Polio Syndrome

Back in the mid-1970s, adults who had recovered from paralytic polio twenty or thirty years earlier were experiencing some strange new symptoms: fatigue, exhaustion, muscle weakness, painful joints, difficulty breathing and swallowing, and sleep problems. What was causing these problems? It seemed as though they were experiencing the effects of polio all over again. It was not until the 1980s that doctors realized that these people were suffering from a condition called post-polio syndrome (PPS).[11] Scientists at the National Institutes of Health defined post-polio syndrome as "the development of new muscle weakness and fatigue in skeletal or in bulbar-controlled muscles, unrelated to any known cause, that begins between twenty-five and thirty years after an acute (severe) attack of paralytic polio."[12]

It is estimated that there are 650,000 polio survivors in the United States today. Studies have shown that about 20 to 40 percent of those who fully recovered from the polio infection many years ago develop post-polio syndrome. That may be as many as 128,000 to 250,000 people who are now showing signs of PPS.[13]

Patients must meet certain criteria before they are diagnosed with PPS. They must have:

- A history of acute paralytic polio in childhood or adolescence.

- New muscle weakness or pain in the muscles and/or joints.

30

- Experienced normal motor functioning for at least ten to fifteen years since recovering from polio.

Why are these symptoms appearing after so many years of being "polio-free?" PPS is not caused by a reactivation of the poliovirus. It does not hide out in the nerves and resurface after many years, like the chickenpox virus does when it causes shingles. Instead, many scientists believe that post-polio syndrome occurs as a result of years of stress on the muscles.

Remember that in helping the body recover from symptoms of polio, healthy nerve fibers sprout new branches to take over the work of the dead nerve cells. After years of being overworked and doing more than their share, the nerve cells are no longer able to support the nerve sprouts, and eventually some of them wither and die. Gradually, the muscle being served by those nerve sprouts continues to weaken. This process is further complicated by the fact that natural aging causes the nerve connections in the body to weaken.[14]

Sadly, many polio survivors, who battled polio many years ago and won, are finding themselves back using wheelchairs or crutches, and those whose breathing muscles lost their function many years ago need to use respirators again.

3

Polio in History

Widespread polio epidemics first started to occur in the early 1900s. People thought they were seeing a strange new illness. This was not true, however. In fact, evidence shows that polio dates back thousands of years, although it was not the same type of devastating disease of epidemic proportions it became in the first half of the twentieth century.

An ancient Egyptian stone engraving, dating back to 1500 B.C., depicts a priest with one withered leg, supporting himself with a staff propped up under his arm. Health experts believe that this depiction suggests the presence of paralytic polio.[1]

Over the centuries, there were other accounts of what seems to be polio. Sir Walter Scott, the author of *Ivanhoe* and other historical novels, was born in 1771. In his memoirs he writes that he had been told that until the age of eighteen months he was a healthy little boy. One morning, however, he woke up with a fever that lasted three days. His parents thought he was just teething, but on the fourth day young Scott was unable to

This three-thousand-year-old stone slab from Egypt, depicting a man with one withered leg, may be the earliest evidence of polio.

move his right leg, even though it looked perfectly normal. "The impatience of a child soon inclined me to struggle with my infirmity," Scott wrote, "and I began by degrees to stand, to walk, and to run." Although his leg remained "much shrunk and contracted," Scott quickly recovered and became "a healthy, high-spirited, and, my lameness apart, a sturdy child."[2]

In a book on childhood diseases published in 1789, an English physician, Michael Underwood, described a condition he called "debility of the lower extremities." Underwood commented that this was not a common disorder and noted that when both legs were paralyzed, "irons to the legs" (i.e., braces) could be used to support the legs and enable the affected children to walk.[3] In the years that followed, there were a few more medical reports of paralysis in children, most likely resulting from polio.

In 1840, Jacob von Heine, a German orthopedist (a specialist in diseases of the bones and joints), made a detailed analysis of a number of paralytic polio cases and wrote the first clear medical description of the disease. Heine described the course of the disease, which has an early stage of fever and pain followed by paralysis, and speculated that it might be contagious. For treatment he recommended exercise, baths, and the use of metal braces.[4] In the mid-1800s, polio was not yet widespread in Europe and North America. The infection was typically seen in infants and very young children. The symptoms were usually mild, with only a few reports of paralysis. Calling attention to how young the patients were (from six months to three years old in the cases he studied), Heine named this disease infantile paralysis in 1843.

Around 1870, André Cornil, a French pathologist (one who studies diseases), performed the first autopsy (a physical examination after death) on a patient who had paralytic polio, paying particular attention to the brain and spinal cord. Cornil's colleague, Jean-Martin Charcot, did a follow-up of this autopsy and discovered that the damaged tissue was found in the part of the spinal cord called the anterior horn, an area containing nerve cells that control muscle movements.[5]

By the late 1800s, polio was becoming more and more common. The first epidemic was reported in 1887 in Stockholm, Sweden. Pediatrician Karl Oskar Medin reported forty-four polio cases in a city that usually had just one to two cases a year. Medin investigated this strange burst of polio cases and classified the different types of paralysis that he saw.

In 1905, a student of Medin's, Swedish pediatrician Ivar Wickman, studied a much larger polio epidemic—more than one thousand cases. Observing his young patients, Wickman discovered that there were actually two forms of the disease. Paralysis occurred in only a small number of cases; there were many more patients with very mild symptoms. Wickman suggested that this was a very contagious disease, and although people with very mild symptoms did not suffer like the other patients, they were still helping to spread the disease to other people.[6]

The first polio epidemic in the United States occurred in 1894, in Rutland, Vermont, affecting 132 people.[7] By the early twentieth century, polio epidemics were a common occurrence in Europe, North America, and Australia. Outbreaks in these areas were occurring every summer to early fall. Before this time, polio affected mostly children. But now, the disease was shifting to include older patients. The disease was different in adults, however. In young children, the disease was generally mild, often going unnoticed, and it usually did not involve paralysis. In young adults, the disease was more serious, and paralysis was more common.[8]

Dirt and Disease

People often associate dirt with disease. Many serious diseases are caused by germs that thrive in unsanitary conditions. But polio is not a disease of filth and poverty. Ironically, polio epidemics are most likely to occur in developed countries.

For centuries, babies had been exposed to the poliovirus present in the environment, but the disease had not caused a widespread problem as it did later on. Exposure to the virus allowed the children to develop an immunity to the disease early in life, and they were protected from getting it again. When the children did develop the illness, the symptoms were usually mild.

However, as industrialized countries such as the United States and Sweden developed better sanitation measures and less crowded living conditions, more and more people went through childhood without ever being exposed to the poliovirus. As a result, people who lived in the developed countries did not develop an immunity through exposure in early childhood. Later exposure led to outbreaks of a more serious form of the disease with crippling effects. In developing countries, where overcrowding and poor sanitation were common, polio was endemic (present in the local populations). But in these situations it was generally a milder disease that did not burst out in frightening widespread epidemics.[9]

In 1916, polio struck twenty-nine thousand people in the United States, killing six thousand of them.[10] The disease stirred up a lot of fear and panic across the country. For much of the early twentieth century, the fear of polio controlled peoples' everyday activities. During the summer months, swimming pools, beaches, playgrounds, and movie theaters were closed during epidemic outbreaks, and schools would not open until the summer epidemic was over.

At this point, polio was accepted as an unfortunate part of life. It was not easy for doctors and family members to watch polio victims with withering limbs. Even worse were patients whose breathing muscles would not work, so that air could not be drawn into their lungs. Unfortunately, these patients often died.

In 1929, however, engineer Philip Drinker and his colleagues at the Harvard School of Public Health were working on a machine that could bring air into the body, allowing the patient to breathe. This contraption was essentially a large metal tank, which covered the patient's body, leaving the head sticking out. Inside the tank, a pump created a partial vacuum, forcing the patient's chest to expand, thus drawing air into the lungs through the nose and mouth. When the pump released the vacuum, the person's chest would relax, expelling air from the body. This machine was first tested on animals. Then it was used to help premature infants breathe. Finally, it was adapted to help young polio patients with respiratory paralysis, and, later, adults as well. The machine proved to be effective, breathing life into these patients who would otherwise not be able to breathe.

Word of the new Drinker respirator spread quickly, and for some years manufacturers could not make the machines fast enough to help everyone who needed them. Philip Drinker got phone calls from all over the world and gave instructions on how to make the devices, which were soon popularly called "iron lungs." Polio patients with respiratory paralysis often had to be transported long distances to the few specialized hospitals equipped with iron lungs. As the supply increased, army airplanes transported the machines to cities and towns where epidemics had broken out. Some hospitals had a staff of engineers working round the clock to keep the iron lungs running. If one broke down, an alarm rang to summon hospital workers who kept the respirator pumping with a hand-operated bellows until the breakdown was repaired.[11]

This photo shows a hospital unit for polio patients at Dr. W. H. Groves Latter-Day Saints Hospital in Salt Lake City, Utah, in 1949. The ward contains three iron lungs, two of which are occupied (right, front and left, rear).

In the 1930s, most health experts believed that the only thing that could be done for paralyzed muscles was to keep them at rest and put them in splints (pieces of wood or some other rigid material) to keep them straight. This opinion changed in 1940 when an Australian nurse, Sister Elizabeth Kenny, arrived in America. She had devised a different kind of therapy for polio survivors: the patients' bodies and limbs were wrapped in hot, moist packs to relieve the pain and muscle spasms, by making the tense muscles relax. Kenny's program also involved stretching the muscles, which strengthened the surrounding muscle fibers. Patients whose nerve cells were only mildly damaged might gradually regain the use of their once withered limbs, although the program was not much help for those whose nerve cells were severely damaged. Kenny's treatments were widely used to help polio patients all over the country.[12]

By the 1940s, it was clear that the disease no longer affected children only, and the term "infantile paralysis" seemed outdated. So in 1947, health experts decided to substitute the scientific name of the disease, poliomyelitis, which was soon shortened to "polio" in newspaper articles and in common speech.[13]

Polio epidemics were increasing every year, crippling thousands. The disease reached its peak in 1952, when 57,879 polio cases were reported to the United States Centers for Disease Control and Prevention (CDC). Scientists were determined to find a way to prevent this devastating disease.[14]

Solving the Mystery

One big advance occurred in 1908 when two scientists from Vienna, Karl J. Landsteiner and his assistant Erwin Popper, discovered what was causing the polio infection. These researchers took spinal cord tissue from a nine-year-old boy who had died of polio and injected small portions of the diseased tissue into various experimental animals. The injections had no apparent effect on rabbits, guinea pigs, or mice. But when the researchers tried the experiment on two monkeys (whose bodies are much more similar to those of humans), the monkeys developed symptoms of polio seventeen days later. Following up these studies, Landsteiner and his colleagues demonstrated that the disease was transmitted by a virus that infects the nervous system. They and other research teams found the virus present in various materials from polio victims, including nasal secretions and samples from the tonsils, the lining of the throat, and lymph nodes from the intestines. Researchers later found the poliovirus present in the blood of animals that were in the early stages of infection.[15]

Monkeys became an important part of polio research. By studying monkeys, for example, scientists showed that the poliovirus attacks the nerve cells in the spinal cord (anterior horn cells) that send signals to control the muscle movements. This discovery confirmed Charcot's findings in the autopsy of a human patient.

Unfortunately, the emphasis on monkey experiments led to a mistaken belief, which wound up delaying progress in developing a way to prevent polio. Rhesus monkeys are very susceptible to polio, but they are infected by way of the respiratory tract, unlike humans who are infected by way of the digestive system. Simon Flexner, an American researcher who was the first to show that polio can be transmitted not only from humans to monkeys but also from one monkey to another, thought that humans caught the disease in the same way as his experimental

Austrian scientist Karl J. Landsteiner (above) and his colleague, Erwin Popper, discovered in 1908 that a virus was causing polio.

A Quirk of Luck

In 1908, Karl J. Landsteiner was still just a junior faculty member at the prestigious University of Vienna in Austria. When he requested monkeys in order to study the transmission of polio, he was not considered important enough to receive any of the expensive New World monkeys available at the university. Instead, he was given a couple of "used" Rhesus monkeys that were left over from another experiment. Ironically, if Landsteiner had had enough clout to rate some "new" monkeys, he never would have made his breakthrough discovery, since New World monkeys are not susceptible to polio![16] With the increased respect won by his successful polio experiments, Landsteiner later went on to make other valuable contributions to medical research, and in 1930 he won a Nobel Prize for the discovery of human blood types.[17]

monkeys. Flexner headed the Rockefeller Institute in New York for three decades starting in 1903, and his opinion was very influential.[18]

Eventually, however, animal research yielded results that were in better agreement with the findings of the Swedish doctors who studied polio in human patients. Scientists found, for example, that certain species of monkeys and also chimpanzees could be infected by mouth (part of the digestive system) when they were fed food contaminated with the poliovirus. In one experiment at Yale University, flies that came in contact with feces from polio patients were then allowed to feed on bananas. Monkeys that later ate the bananas came down with paralytic polio. The disease could also be produced by injecting the animal with infected material from a polio patient who had died, or from a diseased monkey. Polioviruses could be found in an infected animal's throat and also in the feces of a diseased animal days after its exposure to the virus, demonstrating that the virus was actively living and reproducing in its host's digestive tract. All these findings showed that the poliovirus produced an infection that started out in the throat and intestines and later traveled through the blood to the central nervous system.[19]

In a large experiment conducted in 1949, scientists discovered that there were three different types of poliovirus. This meant that a monkey that was immune to one type of poliovirus was not necessarily immune to the other two. These polioviruses were described as type 1, or Brunhilde; type 2, or Lansing; and type 3, or Leon. This discovery removed another stumbling block in the way of developing protection against polio. Before this, researchers had not realized that an effective vaccine would have to provide protection against all three types, rather than only one virus strain.[20]

The Road to Prevention

Researchers had known about vaccinations for over a century. Vaccines can produce an immune reaction in a patient without the severe effects of the disease. The smallpox vaccine, for instance, was developed by Edward Jenner in the late 1700s. To produce this vaccine, Jenner used a virus that produced a milder illness (cowpox) but was similar enough to the smallpox virus to stimulate the body's natural defenses against it. Researchers hoped to imitate this process for polio, perhaps by using a weakened but still "live" form of the poliovirus that did not cause paralysis. Another possible approach would be to use polioviruses that had been killed by heat or chemicals. Killed viruses could not cause any disease symptoms, but they could still stimulate the body's immune defenses.

Early attempts in developing a polio vaccine were disastrous. In 1936, a group of researchers from New York, headed by Dr. John Kolmer, created a vaccine that used a weakened form of poliovirus, taken from the spinal cords of diseased monkeys. After the vaccine was tested and seemed to work in monkeys, Kolmer used it to inoculate, or vaccinate, human children. He then sent out thousands of doses of the vaccine to other doctors around the country. Some of the vaccinated children became paralyzed, and some even died. It was believed that the vaccine, which contained live poliovirus, was the cause of the disaster. Apparently the virus had not been weakened enough.

That same year, another group of researchers, headed by Dr. Maurice Brodie, developed a vaccine using a killed strain of poliovirus. The results were not as devastating as Kolmer's had been, but the vaccine was not effective. This was before scientists knew there were three different types of poliovirus. These early experiments were considered careless, and their safety measures were inadequate.[21]

The Kolmer fiasco made both the public and researchers fearful of using a live vaccine against polio, and it channeled research efforts toward developing a killed vaccine. It was evident that more knowledge about polio was needed before it would be safe to experiment on humans, and, in addition, some practical problems had to be worked out. Before a useful vaccine could be developed, scientists had to be able to grow the poliovirus in a cell or tissue culture rather than inside the body of a live animal. The amount of material that can be taken from an animal is very limited, and could not be the basis of mass production of a vaccine for immunizing millions of humans. Another obstacle that had to be overcome was the fact that up to that time, the poliovirus could be grown only in nerve tissue. This medium would not be suitable for a vaccine, because bits of nerve tissue in the injected material can provoke allergic reactions that might damage the brains of the vaccinated children.

A breakthrough came in 1948, when Harvard researchers John Enders, Thomas Weller, and Frederick Robbins developed a method for growing the poliovirus in a tissue culture, using a solution made from monkey kidneys. These scientists were able to grow, measure, and change viruses in test tubes and culture dishes without having to inject the virus into an animal's body. Now, using material from a single monkey, researchers were able to produce hundreds of times as much virus as they could in the monkey's own body. Enders, Weller, and Robbins published a paper on their findings in 1949, and they received a Nobel Prize for their work in 1954.[22]

Jonas Salk, a virologist (doctor or researcher who studies viruses), had produced killed-virus vaccines for influenza during and after World War II. Salk was working on a killed vaccine for polio. By 1952, Salk believed that his vaccine was effective. Once injected, the killed vaccine would be able to provoke an immune response that would protect the body against polio if it was exposed to the virus in the future. Salk tested the vaccine on a number of children, including his own, and then set his aim for widespread use. In a large study sponsored by the National

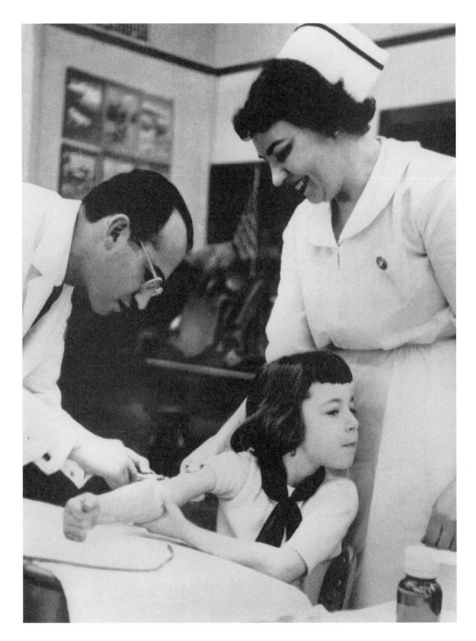

Dr. Jonas Salk, left, injects a girl with his polio vaccine.

Foundation for Infantile Paralysis in 1954, almost 2 million children were injected with Salk's polio vaccine. The vaccine proved to be effective, and in 1955 Salk's vaccine was licensed by the United States government for use.[23]

Salk's polio vaccine brought relief and enthusiasm in many communities of the United States and in other countries, especially those that were hit hardest by the disease. Mass vaccination programs were set up in many areas. As a result, there was a sharp decrease in polio cases.

However, an upsetting setback occurred in April 1955, when a bad batch of vaccines manufactured by Cutter Laboratories in California got into circulation. As a result of the immunizations using this batch, 204 children came down with polio; 153 were paralyzed, and 11 died.[24] In some cases, the victims had not received the injections themselves; they were siblings or playmates of children who had been vaccinated. This meant that at least some doses of the vaccine contained live poliovirus, capable of transmitting the infection. The polio cases and deaths due to the Cutter vaccine were widely publicized; nevertheless, this time the idea of polio vaccination was not set aside. It was quickly established that this setback was just an isolated incident, not a fatal flaw in the concept, and the faulty processing methods that had failed to kill the virus were corrected.

Overall, the first vaccination effort was a stunning success. The killed vaccine reduced the number of polio cases by 80 percent in some areas where everyone was vaccinated.[25] In 1960, the number of new polio cases had dropped to 3,190. The number dropped again to 1,312 cases in 1961, and to only 910 cases in 1962.[26]

Meanwhile, another virologist had been working on a somewhat different approach to a vaccine to prevent polio. Dr. Albert Sabin had been involved in polio research since 1931 and had developed vaccines for other diseases during World War II.[27] Sabin believed that more effective and longer-lasting protection would be provided by an attenuated (weakened) live vaccine. The vaccine that Sabin developed in the late 1950s contained a living, but weakened form of the poliovirus. Sabin and his colleagues selected from forms of polioviruses that did not attack nerve cells but could still infect the intestines. That way the vaccine would trigger the production of antibodies without actually causing any serious symptoms of the disease.

After smaller-scale tests of his vaccine (including the immunization of his own children), Sabin conducted a massive test in Russia, in areas where there were polio epidemics. His vaccine was given orally (by mouth), which made it easy to administer. Within the next two years, 77 million Russians received Sabin's oral vaccine, and it was considered effective by world health experts. In 1960, the Sabin vaccine was licensed for use in the United States.

Vaccination programs were set up across the country, using the oral vaccine in a sweet liquid form or soaked into a sugar cube. Within the next five years, there was a general change in the form of polio vaccination used in the United States. American doctors preferred to use Sabin's oral vaccine instead of Salk's injected vaccine, because of its convenience and the belief that it would provide more complete and lasting protection.[28] The oral vaccine was used in most other countries of the world, as well. Polio cases were disappearing at dramatic rates in developed countries. The last wild case of polio (that is, illness resulting from infection by poliovirus present in the environment) in the United States occurred in 1979. And in August 1991, the last wild case of polio in the Western Hemisphere occurred in a young Peruvian boy.[29]

Dr. Albert Sabin had been involved in polio research since 1931 and developed vaccines for other diseases during World War II. In the late 1950s he began to develop an oral polio vaccine, which was licensed for use in the United States in 1960.

Since the first efforts to develop a polio vaccine, a controversy has continued to rage on the relative merits of the live, attenuated polio vaccine vs. the killed-virus vaccine. Though both vaccines have been considered generally safe and effective, there has been growing concern about using the live vaccine. During the 1990s, about eight to ten people in the United States were infected with the poliovirus each year, after receiving the live oral vaccine.

4

Diagnosing and Treating Polio

It was homecoming day at school in September 1949 when twelve-year-old Peg Schulze noticed a muscle twitching in her left thigh. She tried to stop it with her hand, but it just kept jerking around uncontrollably. Later that morning, Peg's legs suddenly became weak, and she fell to the floor. She thought she was getting sick because two days earlier, she had developed a sore throat and a headache; now she felt weak, and her back hurt.

After school, Peg walked the twelve blocks it took to get home. Later, her mother felt Peg's forehead and said, "You feel hot." She sent her daughter to bed. A few hours later, Peg woke up with a stiff neck. Her back hurt a lot, and she also had terrible muscle spasms and could not straighten her legs or toes.

The next morning, Peg's mother took her daughter's temperature—it was 102 degrees Fahrenheit (nearly 39 degrees Celsius). The doctor came to the house to examine Peg and advised her mother to sponge her with a cool, wet cloth to bring down the fever. Peg slept most of the day and vomited when she woke up at

51

midnight. When the doctor came back the next morning, Peg's temperature was still 102 degrees Fahrenheit. He tapped her knees with a rubber hammer, but instead of producing the expected knee-jerk reflex, her legs did not move. Then he ran his fingernail across Peg's foot. Although it hurt a lot, she could not pull it away. The same thing happened with her other foot.

The doctor asked Peg's parents to bring her to the hospital so she could be tested. There, the doctor inserted a needle into Peg's spinal column and withdrew some fluid. The laboratory analyzed the spinal fluid right away, and the doctor spoke to Peg's parents when the results of the spinal tap test came in. Peg had polio. When they told Peg, all she could envision were March of Dimes posters showing polio patients in wheelchairs or wearing heavy iron leg braces.

Peg was taken to a hospital that specialized in polio patients, the Sheltering Arms Hospital in the nearest large city, Minneapolis, Minnesota. She was brought into a private room in the isolation ward. Here only patients and their nurses and doctors, who wore masks, were allowed to enter. Peg fell asleep, and when she woke up, she could no longer move her arms and legs— she was paralyzed from the neck down. The doctor came in and examined Peg. He lifted Peg's arm and asked her to hold it in the air. When he let go of her wrist, it just dropped down to the bed. The doctor also noticed that her breathing muscles were weak.

Over the next few days, Peg's fever stayed at 102 degrees Fahrenheit, and she had increasing trouble breathing and swallowing. The doctor told her that she had all three types of polio: spinal polio, which causes paralysis in the arms and legs; respiratory polio, which affects the breathing muscles; and bulbar polio, which causes difficulty in talking or swallowing. Sheltering Arms Hospital specialized in rehabilitating polio patients and was not equipped to treat patients with severe breathing problems who might need an artificial respirator. So Peg was transferred to University Hospital, which had the staff and equipment needed.

An oxygen tent was set up for Peg in the hospital. This was a sheet of plastic held in place by a frame, three feet from her face, in which oxygen was released from a cylinder of the compressed gas. This readily available oxygen would help her breathe easier. She felt fortunate not to need the infamous iron lung.

Peg's high fever continued for over a week; her whole body ached, and swallowing was becoming more difficult. She could not eat for a week until a nurse bent the rules and let Peg drink her favorite treat, a chocolate milkshake. (Milk is usually considered dangerous for polio patients because it can cause choking.) Peg's temperature finally broke, and her condition improved. Soon she could swallow more easily, and the aches and pains faded away. She also no longer needed the oxygen tent. Finally, Peg could be moved out of isolation. She says chocolate milk saved her life.

Now that Peg was out of the critical stage, it was time to begin the treatments of hot packs and muscle-stretching exercises. The nurse took large woolen cloths soaked in hot water and laid them on Peg's back, arms, and legs. At first, the hot packs felt like torture, burning her skin. But as they cooled down, she could feel her tight muscles relaxing in the warm, moist heat. The hot pack treatments were continued twice a day for the rest of her stay at University Hospital.

The hot packs were only the first part of the treatment. The second part involved special stretching exercises. These are important because during the time the patient has a fever, along with muscle spasms, the muscles tighten. Later, the muscles have to be stretched back to normal before they can regain their strength.

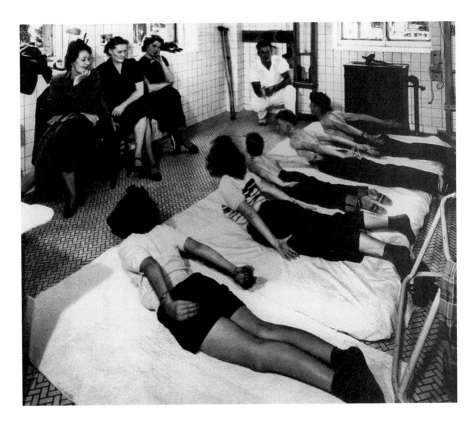

In the center rear of the photo a physiotherapist is giving directions to convalescing polio patients on how to do their stretching exercises. On the left, the patients' mothers watch.

The nurse had to move Peg's limbs into various positions that made Peg scream in pain. After a couple of weeks of "torture time," as she called it, Peg managed to move the fingers of her left hand. Her right hand moved too. Over the next few days, her condition greatly improved. She could use both hands and her arms, and she could sit up. Soon she could also move her legs. With the aid of intensive physical therapy, Peg's arms and legs were getting stronger and stronger. Finally, in mid-October, Peg was well enough to be sent back to Sheltering Arms Hospital to continue her recuperation. To her delight, soon after her arrival the hot pack treatments were replaced by long soaks in a hot bath, which relaxed the muscles and were much less painful than the hot packs.

Peg's three roommates at the hospital were girls of about her age, who were also recovering from polio. Peg soon noticed that none of the other girls had visitors. The family of one girl lived so far away that they had been able to make the trip to Minneapolis only twice in the seven months the girl had been at Sheltering Arms. Another girl's parents could not arrange to have someone take over their chores on the farm so they could make the long trip. The third girl had been abandoned by her family shortly after she first got polio at the age of three, when they learned that she would not regain the full use of her leg; they did not want to

A polio patient soaks in a large whirlpool tub and receives treatment from a physiotherapist in 1949.

be burdened by a "cripple." Peg's parents, who fortunately lived close enough—and cared enough—to visit her every week, befriended Peg's roommates and began bringing them gifts. As Peg continued her recovery, her parents also brought her schoolbooks and the class assignments for each week. Studying on her own, in addition to the couple of hours a day of schooling she received at the hospital, Peg was able to keep up with her classmates back at home.

Meanwhile, Peg worked hard with her physical therapy. Eventually, she graduated from a wheelchair to walking sticks. These were short crutches, each with an iron ring at the top, into which the patient's arms were inserted up to just below the elbow. Like the other patients, Peg was given her own pair of walking sticks, carefully fitted to her height to help her keep her balance and develop good posture. By Christmas, Peg was doing well enough to be allowed to go home for a two-day visit. In February 1950, five months after she first got sick, Peg was ready to go home for good. She was instructed to continue exercising there. Eventually, she conquered polio and learned to walk again.

But forty years later, Peg started to experience fatigue, muscle aches, foot cramps, and back pain. She was saddened to find out that she had post-polio syndrome. Peg would have to battle the effects of polio all over again. Now she is back in physical therapy, trying to manage this disabling disease.[1]

Peg's story illustrates how polio was diagnosed and treated over fifty years ago. Basically, the same techniques are used today, except some new medications have been added to help ease the pain and relax muscle spasms.

Confusing the Signs

Unlike chicken pox and measles, which usually have unmistakable symptoms, polio cases often go unnoticed. Often the symptoms are subtle, and they also resemble the symptoms of other illnesses. A patient who develops a fever, headache, and muscle aches will probably assume it is the flu. For many people, these "flu-like symptoms" go away in less than a week, and the patient is unaware of having polio. But if the symptoms worsen instead of getting better, as we saw in Peg's case, it is time to see the doctor.

It May Look Like Polio, but It's Not

Polio belongs to the family of enteroviruses, which include intestinal diseases that can cause damage to the nervous system. So what appears to be polio may actually be another disease, with similar symptoms. An illness called Guillain-Barré syndrome causes muscle weakness or paralysis. This ailment sometimes develops one to three weeks after a mild viral infection or after an immunization. Like polio, Guillain-Barré syndrome attacks nerves that control muscles in various parts of the body. The muscles that control swallowing and breathing may also be affected, forcing the patient to use a respirator. Most patients recover the use of their muscles, but it may take up to a year. Some Guillain-Barré patients, however, are left with weakened muscles for the rest of their lives.[2]

Testing For Polio

In order to distinguish polio from other illnesses, the doctor must take samples from the patient's throat and feces to be analyzed in the laboratory. A technician then places the samples in a suitable culture and tries to grow and identify the poliovirus.

The doctor also performs a lumbar puncture or spinal tap to get a sample of the patient's cerebrospinal fluid (CSF). CSF is a clear fluid that flows through the space surrounding the brain and spinal cord. This fluid contains glucose (sugar), proteins, and certain chemicals. It does not normally contain red blood cells or very many white blood cells.

To prepare for the spinal tap procedure, the patient must lie down on his or her side and curl up into a ball so that there are spaces between the vertebrae of the spine. The area of the lower spine is numbed with an anesthetic, or pain-killing medicine. The doctor then inserts a small, hollow needle between two vertebrae and sucks up a sample of the spinal fluid. This fluid is then examined under a microscope.

Abnormal test results may show an increase in the number of white blood cells. This symptom indicates an inflammation of the spinal cord, a sign of meningitis, and it is often associated with polio infection. An increased level of proteins and slight pressure on the brain are also indications of polio.[3]

A Misguided Idea

There is no perfect treatment for polio. There are no drugs that can stop nerve cells from being damaged, nor are any drugs available to repair those already damaged. But effective treatment of the symptoms can reduce the devastating effects of the disease.

Before the 1940s, polio patients were not treated effectively. The widely held belief was that paralyzed muscles should be rested and immobilized to prevent further damage. Muscle spasms caused patients' arms and legs to bend, and without treatment, these limbs might stay bent permanently. Therefore, doctors routinely placed paralyzed limbs in casts and splints to keep them straight. Unfortunately, when the casts or splints came off, the limbs could not move at all, and the paralysis was often permanent. Remember that muscles that are not used get weaker and will eventually atrophy, or wither away. Sometimes, doctors even used splints for patients with mild muscle weakness, which only worsened the condition as atrophy set in. Muscles that were not affected by polio also shrank from disuse. Thus, the idea of immobilization for managing paralyzed muscles was not only wrong, it was harmful. The longer effective treatment is delayed, the more likely it is that paralysis will become permanent.[4]

A Polio Pioneer

Polio treatment was revolutionized in 1940, when Australian nurse Elizabeth Kenny arrived in the United States with her own ideas for treating paralyzed muscles.

Elizabeth Kenny had been interested in learning about muscles since she was a teenager, when she broke her wrist after falling off a horse. At that time her doctor, Aeneas McDonnell, showed her textbooks on muscles and how they worked. Kenny was so fascinated that she tried to learn as much as she could. She even set up an exercise program for her younger brother, Bill, who had very weak muscles as a child. The exercises worked so well that eventually he got healthier and stronger.

In 1907, Kenny became a nurse in the remote countryside in Australia, even though she did not have any formal training. There were no telephones and no nearby hospitals. She wanted to help people who could not get to a doctor. Mostly she treated farm injuries and delivered babies. But in 1911, Kenny encountered a condition she had never seen before. On a farm, Kenny examined a two-year-old girl who was in a lot of pain. The child could not straighten out one arm and one leg. Kenny sent a telegram to Dr. McDonnell describing the child's symptoms and asked his opinion. He quickly replied: "It sounds like infantile paralysis. There's no known treatment, so do the best you can with the symptoms presenting themselves."[5]

Kenny believed that the child's pains were caused by muscle spasms. So she used her knowledge about muscles and applied hot, moist rags to the affected muscles. As the heat helped the muscles relax, the little girl stopped crying and fell asleep. Kenny continued to use hot packs to soothe the muscles and massaged the girl's arm and leg until she could straighten them. The little girl eventually recovered without any crippling effects of the disease.

Around that time, twenty children in the area developed polio. Kenny treated six of these children, all of whom recovered fully. She wanted to tell the doctors about her methods, but they would not listen—her ideas were completely opposite to the current practices.

Kenny took a break from treating polio patients when she became a nurse for the Australian Army in World War I. In 1916, Kenny was promoted to head nurse, and was given the title "sister." Sister Kenny, as she became known thereafter, did not return to treating polio patients until 1931, when polio had become a worldwide epidemic.

In 1933, Sister Kenny set up her first polio clinic. She started out with seventeen patients and continued her treatments of hot packs and physical therapy. Eventually, word got out about Kenny's unusual treatments, and people from all over the world came to her clinic. She eventually set up three more clinics and helped hundreds of patients. But still, the Australian medical officials were very critical of Sister Kenny's treatment methods. In a report issued in 1937, it stated that immobilization was the only treatment for polio, and that Kenny's methods would only result in permanently crippling the patients. This negative publicity did not stop patients from flocking to Kenny's clinics.

In 1940, Sister Kenny decided to leave Australia and travel to the United States to see if American doctors would be more accepting of her treatment methods. At first, Sister Kenny was rejected by the National Infantile Paralysis Foundation and the American Medical Association. But she was finally invited by doctors at the University of Minnesota to demonstrate her techniques. The doctors were amazed. Badly crippled patients showed remarkable improvement after Kenny's treatments. Sister Kenny was so successful that a number of Minneapolis doctors asked for her help with their polio patients. Soon Sister Kenny's methods were widely accepted.

In December 1942, the Sister Kenny Institute was established in Minneapolis to teach therapists about Kenny's theories and methods. More and more doctors abandoned the idea of immobilization, and by 1947, more than ten thousand splints were abandoned and sold for scrap. Her methods were eventually accepted all over the world—including Australia. Sister Kenny's treatments continued to help thousands of polio patients, even after she died in 1952.[6]

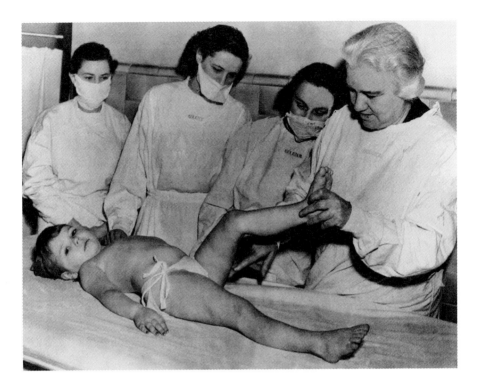

Australian nurse Elizabeth Kenny, who later became known as Sister Kenny, invented new therapies to deal with the symptoms of polio. These included heat packs, massage, and stretching exercises. Here Kenny, far right, demonstrates her techniques at the Sister Kenny Institute in 1942.

Today, the principles that guided Sister Kenny in developing her treatments are used in rehabilitative medicine around the world. These techniques help patients with injuries, as well as those affected by muscle-related illnesses such as Guillain-Barré syndrome and polio. Now that post-polio syndrome is becoming more prevalent, polio survivors are seeking relief for the recurrence of their muscle problems. In addition to hot packs and stretching exercises, doctors also recommend taking pain-relievers, such as ibuprofen, to ease the muscle aches and pains.

Help with Breathing

Sister Kenny believed that her hot pack treatments could benefit even patients with respiratory polio, whose breathing muscles were paralyzed. She opposed the use of iron lungs, which she called "torture chambers." She felt that patients immobilized in an iron lung became dependent on the machine and would have more difficulty recovering their muscle function. In one case she even had a young patient removed from an iron lung against doctors' orders. She then stayed up all night nursing him with hot packs until the spasms in his respiratory muscles were relieved. Many doctors did not share Kenny's extreme views; and in the case of bulbar polio, which affects nerves in the brain stem that control the breathing process, even Sister Kenny reluctantly acknowledged the need for a respirator.[7]

For many polio patients, respiratory paralysis is only temporary, and the respirator is a lifesaving stopgap measure that keeps them breathing until they have recovered enough to breathe on their own. But some patients never do regain the ability to breathe independently and remain dependent on a respirator for the rest of their lives.

Fortunately, respirators have come a long way since the cumbersome iron lungs of the mid-1900s. Completely immobilized in the huge, noisy metal cylinder, polio patients with respiratory paralysis were confined full-time to a hospital room that they could see only upside down by using a mirror in the ceiling. By the 1960s, however, a more portable breathing device, the cuirass respirator, was available. An airtight, dome-shaped fiberglass shell was strapped over the patient's chest and abdomen and connected by a hose to a pump. It worked in the same way as an iron lung, using alternating negative pressure to draw air into the patient's lungs and force it out again a thousand times an hour, but it allowed the patient to lie in a regular bed and even sit in a wheelchair. This device greatly expanded paralyzed patients' opportunities for interacting with the world and participating in many aspects of "normal" life.

The Story of John Prestwich

One polio patient who has made the most of these opportunities is an Englishman named John Prestwich, who holds the Guinness world record for the longest time spent continuously on a mechanical respirator.

In 1955, seventeen-year-old John Prestwich was serving in the British Merchant Navy when his ship docked in Corpus Christi, Texas. While he was helping to prepare the ship for unloading, he began to feel ill. Dizzy and "wobbly," he reported in sick to his first officer and went to his bunk for a nap. When he woke up, he was terrified. He could not move at all, not even to lift his head off the pillow. Late that evening, another seaman found him there and got the ship's chief officer to call the medical authorities. When Prestwich woke up again, he could see the doctor, the captain, and other people crowded around him. Later, he recalls, people were staring down at him, as he was carried off the ship on a stretcher. Prestwich woke up in an iron lung in a Corpus Christi hospital. He had polio. Not only was he totally paralyzed from the chin down, but the polio infection had also damaged his breathing mechanism. He could not breathe without the aid of the iron lung.

Prestwich was not expected to live, and his parents back in England were notified by telegram. With the aid of a priest and a London newspaper, *The Daily Mirror*, his mother flew to Texas to be with him. She helped with the nursing duties and slept each night in a bed next to her son's iron lung. After three months, the United States Air Force flew Prestwich to London. His nurses in Corpus Christi had bought him a pair of pale blue pajamas to wear for the trip, to match the pale blue color of his iron lung.

Back in England, at the Royal Free Hospital in London, Prestwich was very ill for nearly two years. Since polio does not damage the sensory nerves, he was in terrible pain from his atrophying muscles. He recalls that at one point the pain faded away and everything began to get dark and quiet. He sensed that he was dying, but he did not want to give up; "I was too interested in what was going on tomorrow," he says. Gradually he began to feel better. He even asked a physical therapist working with him, "When I start moving, which part of me will start moving first?" There was an embarrassed silence, during which Prestwich realized he might never move again.

As Prestwich's physical and emotional condition gradually improved, he began to use a positive-pressure respirator for short periods. This was a portable device that forced air into his lungs through a mouthpiece. It allowed him to lie in a regular bed, sit in a wheelchair, and even to go outdoors if he had the aid of an attendant who would push the chair. However, since the respirator operated by electricity, he could not venture far from a power supply. Because he had been lying flat on his back in the iron lung for so long, his wasted limbs were locked in place, and it was extremely painful when the nurses moved them into different positions. Venturing out of the hospital was also embarrassing at first, when people who saw him stared and whispered.[8]

More than forty years later, John Prestwich is still alive and totally paralyzed. He still needs a respirator twenty-four hours a day to remain alive. He has a portable ventilator built into a combination wheelchair/bed that allows him to go shopping, travel,

Minutes from Death

Life on a respirator is precarious. The patient is always at the mercy of mechanical or electrical breakdowns that might stop the life-sustaining pump. Without someone there round-the-clock to cope with such emergencies, the patient could die after just a few minutes. However, John Prestwich was taught the technique of "frog breathing," using his tongue and upper neck muscles to swallow air into his lungs. He speculates that by using this trick, he could survive for ten or fifteen minutes without a mechanical breathing aid.

When Prestwich first began venturing further from the hospital on short trips, using a portable positive-pressure respirator, he had a few close calls. Without an electricity supply, the respirator had to be pumped by hand, and one day at the movies, the nurse accompanying Prestwich became so absorbed in the film that she forgot to pump! On another trip the hand-pumped bellows came loose from the base unit. Eventually, Prestwich found a firm that built him a battery-operated respirator.[9] This device enabled him to travel further afield—visits to the seashore on the south coast of England and even a day trip to Paris. Newspaper reporters who had followed him around all day bought him a drink at the top of the Eiffel Tower.

Infections, even a cold, are also life-threatening. A person whose breathing muscles are paralyzed cannot cough and thus cannot clear mucus out of the airways. So the slightest infection sends Prestwich back to the hospital for a stay in an iron lung. Today's models can be rotated face down and tilted into the best position for fluids to drain out of the patient's nose and mouth, and they are equipped with airtight portholes fitted with rubber seals, through which a respiratory therapist can thump the patient's back to help loosen accumulations of mucus in the lungs.[10]

and go to polo matches. The motorized chair/bed, designed and built by a good friend and neighbor, retired computer engineer Jarlath Pattinson, brought Prestwich a new degree of freedom at the end of 1999. For the first time in forty-four years, he was able to move himself from one place to another without relying on another person. The chair/bed is battery-powered and can be controlled by breathing through a tube, using a sip/puff switch that permits Prestwich to drive around, steering with puffs of air. After his first ride on the new chair/bed, Prestwich commented, "Modern technology has liberated me from the prison of dependency to which polio had condemned me."[11]

Modern technology also allows Prestwich to communicate with people all over the world by phone, fax, and Internet. (He

John Prestwich drives himself on his motorized chair/bed on September 26, 1999. He drives it by the sip and puff method.

controls his computer by speaking into a microphone, using speech-to-text software.) Many devices in Prestwich's home are automated. He uses a series of whistled codes to activate his speakerphone, sit himself up or recline in his chair/bed, control his TV, video, and stereo, turn lights on and off, and open his front door. When Prestwich entered the Guinness Book of Records as the longest survivor on a mechanical respirator, reporters asked his next-door neighbor's young daughter why he was so special. "He's the only man in the whole world who can answer the front door by whistling," she declared.[12]

5

Preventing Polio

In 1975, Kay McNeary and her two young children were looking forward to spending Christmas with relatives in Minnesota. They hopped on a bus and headed out of Seattle. During the trip, Kay was uncomfortable—she had a headache, she felt warm, and she had pains in her legs, mostly behind her knees. She figured she had strained her muscles playing touch football two days earlier.

As Kay and her children were getting closer to their destination, her legs hurt even more than before. They finally arrived in St. Paul two days later, and Kay was limping as she got off the bus. At her parents' home, Kay decided to take it easy, so she took a hot bath, and then lay down. The next time she tried to get up, she could not move her legs at all. On Christmas Eve, Kay's legs were paralyzed.

Kay had paralytic polio. This happened during a time when Americans supposedly no longer had to worry about polio, now that vaccinations were readily available. In fact, Kay had contracted the disease as a result of a vaccination that was supposed to protect people against it.

A month earlier, Kay's baby daughter had been given a dose of oral polio vaccine, which contains a weakened but still active form of the virus. Very rarely, the virus may mutate, or change, to a form that can infect nerve tissue, and spread to unprotected people. In Kay's case, she probably contracted the disease when she changed her baby's diapers, which most likely contained reactivated virus particles.

Kay was angry that she had not been given a choice when her daughter was given the polio vaccine. She had not been told that there are two types of polio vaccines: the oral polio vaccine (OPV), which contains a weakened but live form of the virus; and the inactivated polio vaccine (IPV), which contains a killed or inactivated virus. In the United States, the live vaccine has been considered the "vaccine of choice," even though it carries a small risk of actually causing the disease. As far as Kay was concerned after her disastrous experience, that small risk mattered. She wanted to make her concerns public, so she sued both the company that manufactured the vaccine and the public health agencies responsible for administering it. In 1982, Kay won her legal battle, and a Seattle jury awarded her $1.1 million in damages.[1]

Live Polio Vaccine vs. Killed Polio Vaccine

What makes a vaccine effective? The vaccine must be able to trigger an immune response in the body without actually causing the disease. The body produces antibodies against the disease, which then protect it from future exposure to the disease germs. Both the live and killed polio vaccines are effective vaccines. So why do medical experts prefer to use the live vaccine, even though there may be a safer way?

Before we can understand this dilemma, we need to consider the advantages and disadvantages of the live and killed polio vaccines.

The live vaccine is taken orally, which makes it easier to administer to patients, especially children. The vaccine virus travels into the intestines, produces antibodies, and thus provides the body with long-lasting immunity. But that is not all. This live but weakened virus is shed in the mouth and stool for a few weeks after the vaccination. Therefore, it may then be spread to nonvaccinated people, giving them immunity to the disease as well. The more people in a community who are immune to a disease, the less chance that the germ causing it will find susceptible hosts and spread to others. This is called the herd effect, and it provides some protection not only for the people vaccinated but also for the rest of the community.

A disadvantage of the oral vaccine is that it cannot be given to people with weakened immune systems, such as people with AIDS or cancer patients going through chemotherapy. Since the vaccine does contain a live virus, it can cause the disease in these people. It also cannot be given to family members or friends of those susceptible people, since the virus can be shed in the feces and mouth, and can then be transferred to the susceptible family member.

In some cases, the virus mutates as it passes through the body, producing an active, disease-causing form. When this happens, active viruses are shed; they may be transferred to other people and produce the disease. If mutation to the virulent form occurs before the immune defenses against polio have been fully built up, a person who received the live vaccine could, in rare cases, also develop the paralytic form of the disease.

There are three conditions that will determine whether or not the mutated vaccine virus will cause the disease. First, it depends on how virulent the mutated virus is. The second important factor is how strong the person's immune system is—whether it has the ability to fight against the virus. Third, whether the disease develops depends on the amount of exposure to the active virus. For example, a mother like Kay, who changed her child's diapers a number of times a day, would be exposed repeatedly to larger amounts of the virus than a child who has a single brief contact with a playmate.

The killed vaccine, on the other hand, does not contain a living virus and therefore, cannot spread the disease. But the killed vaccine must be given as a shot, which makes it more difficult to administer to patients, especially children.

The killed virus gets into the bloodstream and stimulates the body to produce antibodies that will kill off any future invasion of poliovirus before it can get into the nervous system. The person given the killed polio vaccine is then protected against the disease. But a person who has received this polio shot does not shed the virus, and thus cannot pass on immunity to unvaccinated people.

The killed vaccine is much more effective today than it was when Jonas Salk first developed it in 1955. Today's vaccine is more potent and gives better long-lasting immunity. Studies have shown that the killed vaccine is now just as effective as the live vaccine. However, it provides immunity to paralytic polio but not to infections of cells in the lining of the intestines. This is enough protection for people in the United States and other developed nations where "wild" poliovirus is no longer circulating among the population. It cannot, however, completely wipe out polio in areas where it is still endemic—something that OPV can do.[2]

The SV40 Scare

Between 1955 and 1963, millions of Americans received the polio vaccine, gaining protection against this crippling disease. However, what they did not know at the time was that some batches of IPV and OPV were contaminated with an ape virus called simian virus 40, or SV40.

In 1960, scientists discovered SV40 and soon identified its presence in some batches of the polio vaccine. A year later, studies showed that the virus caused cancer in some rodents, specifically newborn hamsters. By 1962, as many as 98 million people, most of whom were infants and young children, had been given the polio vaccine. About 10 to 30 million of these recipients may have received a vaccine contaminated with SV40. In 1963, efforts to remove SV40 from the polio vaccine were successful—polio vaccines no longer contained SV40.

Viruses that harm animals do not necessarily affect humans. But that is exactly what scientists wanted to find out: can SV40 cause cancer in humans? Recently, using modern techniques, some scientists found SV40-like genes in patients with rare cancers. Other scientists have been unable to confirm these findings because there are no standard laboratory methods for detecting SV40. However, some of these rare cancers with SV40-like genes occurred in small children, who obviously did not receive the polio vaccine in the 1950s and early 1960s. This may mean that there is some source of SV40 in the environment, other than the polio vaccine.

Several studies conducted over the past thirty to forty years have so far not shown any evidence of a link between cancer and SV40. Some of these studies involved several decades of monitoring thousands of people who had received oral or injectable polio vaccine contaminated with SV40. Statistical comparisons of people born during the time when exposure to SV40-containing vaccines was likely and those born before or after this period also showed no difference in the number of rare cancers or in the cancer death rate in general. Scientists will continue to monitor SV40-exposed participants as they age, in case a possible connection to cancer can one day be confirmed.[3]

Dr. Harold Fuerst and Dr. Leona Baumgartner give a polio shot to Elvis Presley in 1956.

When Prevention Efforts Backfire

Thanks to vaccination efforts, no "wild" polio cases have been reported in the United States since 1979. The only polio cases that do occur in this country are those associated with the oral polio vaccine (as well as occasional infections in immigrants from countries where polio is still endemic). About eight to ten vaccine-associated paralytic polio (VAPP) cases are reported each year, resulting from the more than 20 million OPV doses administered.[4]

For years, it seemed that the benefits of the OPV outweighed the risks. Before polio vaccines were available, thousands of polio cases occurred each year. To many people, eight to ten VAPP cases may seem like a small number in comparison. But to people like Kay McNeary, that number is eight to ten too many. Activist groups urged government health agencies to change their polio vaccination policies. Their aim was to eliminate that small, yet important risk, and get health officials to change to the safer, killed polio vaccine.

Changing Vaccination Policies

Since the 1960s, Sabin's oral polio vaccine has been used exclusively in the United States and was responsible for the elimination of wild polio cases in this country. (Some countries

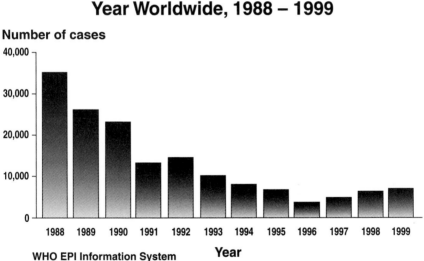

Reported Poliomyelitis Cases by Year Worldwide, 1988 – 1999

Number of cases

WHO EPI Information System   **Year**

This chart released by the World Health Organization shows the decline in polio cases over the years. The apparent increase in the most recent numbers is due to more effective reporting of existing cases.

75

never stopped using Salk's killed vaccine except during epidemics. In Finland, for example, OPV was used to halt an epidemic in the 1980s.) Until recently, children have been routinely given the oral polio vaccine in three doses within the first two years of life, and a booster dose is given when the child starts school. In response to the concerns of public safety, however, health agencies have made some changes in the vaccination policies in an effort to reduce the number of VAPP cases even further.

In 1997, the Centers for Disease Control and Prevention recommended that a mixed schedule of two doses of IPV and two doses of OPV should be used. Normally in VAPP cases, the patients contract the disease after the first or second dose. Therefore, the first two doses would contain the injected killed vaccine and the last two would contain the oral live vaccine. Furthermore, people would be given the option to ask for all OPV or all IPV schedules. According to the CDC, the mixed schedule was designed to reduce, not eliminate future VAPP cases. This would be the first step toward eventually changing the policies to a four-dose IPV schedule. A few VAPP cases still occurred in children who received the OPV thereafter, but no cases were reported in children who received only the killed vaccine.[5]

In January 2000, the CDC recommended that children receive the killed vaccine for all four doses. But the OPV can be used under certain conditions. For instance, a child who travels outside the United States should receive the OPV, since it has the ability to pass on an immunity. OPV will also continue to be used in countries where polio is still endemic, in an effort to eradicate the disease. In addition, doctors would be able to use oral vaccine they had in stock for the third and fourth doses until January 1, 2001.[6] Many people were upset that patients would continue to be at risk for VAPP, just so that doctors would not

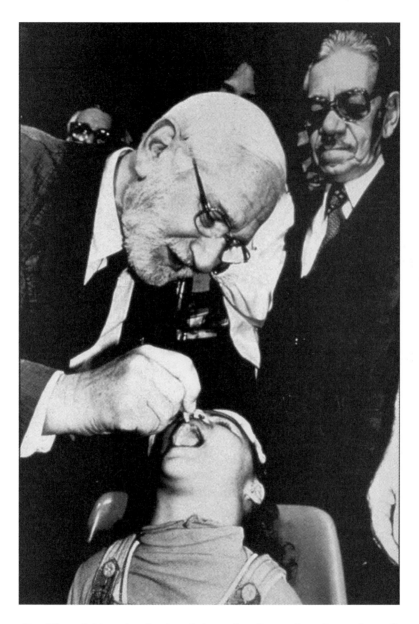

Dr. Albert Sabin, who developed the oral polio vaccine, gives a dose of the vaccine to a child.

lose money for the leftover oral vaccine.[7] Some drug companies reimbursed doctors for their unused polio vaccines to encourage a quicker changeover.

Health officials hope that IPV will eventually be administered along with the standard childhood DPT (diphtheria, pertussis, tetanus) immunizations, which will make polio vaccinations less of a hassle.

6

Polio and Society

Franklin Delano Roosevelt often told people, "I had polio, I was crippled, but I'm a cured cripple now. I may have a limp, but that's all."[1] Although most people knew that Roosevelt had a disability, no one knew how serious his condition really was, even when they saw him up close. He would swing his hips to move forward, only a few feet at a time, while leaning on the arm of a family member or aide. That perception of walking was enough to convince people that FDR was not a "cripple."[2]

Roosevelt often kept his disability hidden from the public. He even built his own wheelchair from a kitchen chair so that it would look more like an ordinary chair.[3] Roosevelt used his wheelchair every single day in the White House. But when he made public appearances, he often wore heavy steel leg braces under his pants. He gave speeches leaning against the podium, or holding onto his crutches or someone's arm.

Roosevelt asked the press not to photograph him in his wheelchair, and they abided by his wishes. Out of the thirty-five thousand photographs taken of FDR, only two of them show him in a wheelchair. One time, when a new press photographer took a picture of FDR being carried from his car to his wheelchair, the secret service and the veteran photographers grabbed the film. Roosevelt felt he had to keep the severity of his disability hidden from the public eye in order to retain the respect of the American people, politicians, and foreign leaders. During the crises of the Great Depression and World War II, he apparently believed that foreign leaders might try to take advantage if they got the impression he was in any way unfit to lead the nation. He also feared the American people might not reelect him.[4]

Roosevelt was not always so private about his condition. He felt at home at Warm Springs. There he could be himself, just like the other disabled people at the spa. He did not have to pretend his disability did not exist, as he did in public. He felt so comfortable at Warm Springs that he often swam with the disabled children who came there for therapy. He had picnics with them, and freely wore his braces over his pants. The children with polio felt a real connection to Roosevelt—they loved and admired him.[5] He also visited military hospitals and stayed in his wheelchair as an inspiration to the disabled soldiers.[6]

A Controversial Memorial

In May 1997, the Franklin Delano Roosevelt Memorial was opened to the public in Washington D.C. The memorial site covers an area of seven and a half acres between the Potomac River and the rim of the Tidal Basin. It has four outdoor rooms designed to depict Roosevelt's life, one room for each of his four

This is room three of the controversial four-room FDR memorial. A nine-foot sculpture shows FDR with his beloved dog, Fala, at his feet. He sits in a regular chair with small wheels, partially covered by his treasured naval cape. The quotation on the wall is from an address Roosevelt gave to the White House Correspondents' Association.

terms in office. When it was completed, the memorial included three sculptures of Roosevelt, but not one of them showed him in his wheelchair.[7] However, one sculpture does show the president in a normal chair with small wheels, which are partially covered by his cape.[8]

The memorial's opening brought protests from activists for the disabled. They complained that by not including a sculpture of FDR in his wheelchair the artist would be distorting history. Other people felt that since Roosevelt went out of his way to hide his paralysis from the public, depicting him in a wheelchair for public viewing would be a distortion of history.

The activists argued that Roosevelt kept his disability a secret because of public opinion at the time. In the 1930s and 1940s, discrimination against people with disabilities was common. Roosevelt probably feared that he could not gain the respect (and the political support) of the people if they saw his true condition. But times have changed, and people today are more accepting of those with disabilities. Moreover, the fact that FDR's condition did not stand in the way of all that he accomplished, both personally and publicly, has been a great inspiration to many disabled people.

The memorial controversy continued until a decision was finally reached more than a year after discussions had begun. In July 1998, Vice-President Al Gore announced that a statue of Franklin Delano Roosevelt in a wheelchair would be placed in the entrance of the memorial. (The statue was installed and dedicated in January, 2001.) Advocates for the disabled community were very pleased with the decision, claiming it was an important victory for the disabilities rights movement.[9]

Then and Now

If Franklin Delano Roosevelt were president of the United States today, and the media revealed his condition, as they most certainly would feel compelled to do, how would people feel? It seems likely that today people would be more accepting. In fact, the media were quick to report President Bill Clinton's knee injury in March 1997. Newspaper articles even included a picture of Clinton in his wheelchair as his aides lifted him up the steps of an airplane.

Clinton had torn the tendon in his right knee after tripping on a few steps at the home of golf professional Greg Norman. Clinton went to the hospital and soon had surgery to repair the damage. After he left the hospital, Clinton had to use a wheelchair for a couple of weeks. After this incident, the media noticed that certain locations at the White House were inaccessible for people with wheelchairs. To make maneuvering possible, rugs had to be taped down, and obstacles had to be removed. Soon Clinton was able to switch to under-the-arm crutches, which made it easier for him to get around. But they were so awkward and uncomfortable that he traded them in for the kind that wrap around the arm, much like the walking sticks used by polio patients. Advisors were afraid, however, that people would liken his disability to Roosevelt's more serious condition.

In early May, Clinton was strong enough to dedicate FDR's memorial opening. As the president slowly walked around on his crutches, it seemed reminiscent of FDR, sixty years earlier. Although Clinton was often in a lot of pain, his image makers advised him to appear strong and confident during public appearances. Attitudes may have improved, but they have not completely changed.[11]

Changing Times

Attitudes towards people with disabilities were very different during Roosevelt's time than they are today. Back then, there was a general feeling that disabilities should be kept hidden and private, and that the disabled were not fit to be seen in public. Disabilities made people uncomfortable. As Hugh Gallagher, a polio paraplegic (a person paralyzed from the waist down) and disabilities activist recalls, disabled people were "supposed to be invalids, kept upstairs in the bedroom with the shades drawn."[10]

Disabled children went to special schools for crippled children. Disabled people typically were cared for at home and were rarely seen in workplaces or at public entertainments. (Partly this was due to the fact that most public places were not accessible to people in wheelchairs.)

These days, we are slowly bringing disabled people into the mainstream of American society. On July 26, 1990, a law was finally passed to protect people with disabilities, providing them with opportunities to live a productive life. The Americans with Disabilities Act (ADA) prohibits discrimination on the basis of disability in employment, programs, and services provided by state and local governments, as well as services provided by private companies. The ADA also states that disabled persons cannot be denied access to public and commercial facilities, from doctors' offices to restaurants, stores, and sports arenas. Reasonable accommodations must be made for disabled persons, such as wheelchair ramps, automatic doors, and handicapped parking spaces.[12]

Disabled people now live in a world that gives them access to facilities that were once considered off-limits. New mechanical devices make living conditions much more bearable. Motorized wheelchairs, scooters, and stair gliders are providing increased mobility, and built-in computers allow users to operate them with voice commands, whistles, or even puffs of breath. The huge, unwieldy, coffin-like iron lung has shrunk to the size of a portable respirator. Orthopedic braces are now lighter and more comfortable.[13]

The passage of the ADA was a reflection of the shift in people's attitudes. It was no longer felt that those with disabilities should be invisible. Efforts were being made to help them participate in many activities that would have been considered way beyond their capabilities in the past. Today, kids with disabilities are encouraged to engage in wheelchair versions of popular sports, from basketball to hockey. Acceptance has been slower for disabled adults, but pioneers like golf pro JaRo Jones are helping to lead the way to greater sports participation.

In 1993, Jones noticed that when he played golf, his drives were not carrying as far as they used to and he was tiring easily. Eventually, it was discovered that he had post-polio syndrome, a delayed result of a bout of polio he had suffered when he was four years old. Although the muscles in his shoulders and legs were deteriorating, Jones continued to play golf, adapting his game to put less stress on his shoulders and ultimately learning to swing from the golf cart he used to get around the links.

When Jones tried to pursue his longtime dream of competing in the United States Senior Open, the United States Golf Association refused to allow him to use his golf cart to compete. Walking is an important part of the game, they argued, and the cart would give Jones an unfair advantage over the other golfers in the tournament. Jones countered that the cart merely allows him to play.

In May 2000 he sued the USGA, and a federal judge confirmed his right to compete in the Senior Open using his cart. Unfortunately, his score was not good enough to qualify him for the event, but as Jones commented, "After I hit the first tee shot, I knew this wasn't about whether I was going to qualify, but that I was there. When I play golf, I'm not just playing for myself any more."

Jones and his wife are working actively toward bringing other people with disabilities into golf. They travel throughout the country, teaching special golf techniques to amputees, cancer survivors, and other people with physical disabilities.[14]

Although great progress has been made in the disabilities movement since the ADA was passed, there is still a long way to go. Out of the estimated 30 million disabled Americans of working age, nearly half of them are still unemployed.[15]

Bearing the Burden

A health crisis, particularly the kind of long-term, ongoing crisis that results from a chronic disease or a severe physical disability, places a heavy burden on a patient's family and the community. There are worries about finances, especially if the problem is not covered by health insurance, or if the insurance coverage runs out. In countries such as Great Britain, with universal health care, taxes ultimately pay for people's medical expenses. In the United States, private charities and government programs such as Medicaid and Medicare help to fill the gap when family resources are not enough. Family members often must act as caregivers—a physically and emotionally exhausting role. Recently, health experts and legislators have been giving increasing attention to the need to provide support for caregivers, as well as for the ill and disabled.[16]

Barbie's Friend Gets a Wheelchair

Mattel, a major toy manufacturer, took a big step in helping to foster public acceptance of the disabled. In 1997, Becky, a doll who uses a wheelchair, was introduced as one of Barbie's friends.

Building new attitudes toward disabilities must start with children. Toys help to shape children's attitudes. To some degree, they reflect the "real world" that the child lives in. Having dolls with disabilities can help the child accept physical limitations matter-of-factly, without prejudice.[17]

Love Bloomed in the Polio Ward

John Prestwich, world record holder as the longest survivor on a mechanical respirator, has shown that a severely disabled person can retain a keen interest and active participation in life. He even fell in love, married, and became a homeowner while totally paralyzed from the neck down and dependent on a respirator.

Maggie Biffin, an occupational therapist, entered his life in 1961, when she was assigned to provide Prestwich with "diversional therapy"—something to keep him occupied. She taught him to sign his name and paint, holding a brush in his mouth and controlling it with his tongue, jaw, and face muscles. She also read to him and helped take him on outings. Soon Maggie began to stay on in the evenings, listening to records with John and sharing snacks with him. As they fell more deeply in love, their relationship seemed hopeless. John had no money, no prospects of a job, and needed twenty-four-hour-a-day nursing care. But Maggie continued to visit John three evenings a week, sometimes staying so late that she missed her bus home.

An unexpected windfall solved their problem. In 1971, John's uncle developed cancer and, knowing he did not have long to live, gave John the deed to a small rental property. With the sale of part of the property and the income from the rest, John now had enough money to buy a cottage and live outside the hospital. He and Maggie were married in December 1971, and since then she has been both his wife and his full-time caregiver. They live a varied and interesting life, putting nine thousand miles a year on their converted minibus as they shop, visit with friends, and attend polo matches. Publicity about John's life as a polio survivor has resulted in meetings with a number of celebrities, including members of the British royal family. John has also enjoyed reunions with a number of people from his past, including the seaman who served with him and persuaded the ship's officer to call the doctor when John first became ill, and the nurses who cared for him during the early years.[18]

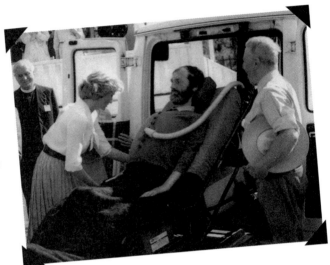

John Prestwich is greeted in 1986 by Diana, Princess of Wales, (left) at the prizegiving ceremony after the polo finals of the Queen's Cup.

John and Maggie Prestwich at home. John whistles into the microphone on his collar to operate his environmental control system.

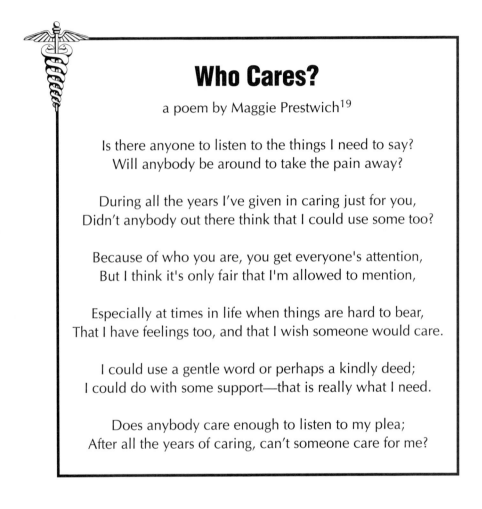

Who Cares?

a poem by Maggie Prestwich[19]

Is there anyone to listen to the things I need to say?
Will anybody be around to take the pain away?

During all the years I've given in caring just for you,
Didn't anybody out there think that I could use some too?

Because of who you are, you get everyone's attention,
But I think it's only fair that I'm allowed to mention,

Especially at times in life when things are hard to bear,
That I have feelings too, and that I wish someone would care.

I could use a gentle word or perhaps a kindly deed;
I could do with some support—that is really what I need.

Does anybody care enough to listen to my plea;
After all the years of caring, can't someone care for me?

7

Polio and
the Future

Humans are the only animals responsible for the spread of polio in the environment, and the poliovirus cannot survive very long outside the human body. Therefore, scientists believe that if we can eliminate the ability of humans to act as hosts by immunizing susceptible people, the poliovirus will quickly die out. Then the disease will ultimately be eliminated. Thus, scientists hope to achieve worldwide eradication of polio in much the same way as they did for smallpox, the first and only disease to be eradicated from the world.

Smallpox was probably the most destructive disease in history, a worldwide plague that evolved from a mild childhood disease in the sixteenth century and killed millions in frequent epidemics in the eighteenth to twentieth centuries.[1] The development in 1796 of a safe vaccine to protect people from the smallpox virus led to its ultimate conquest.[2] By the 1940s, mandatory vaccination programs had eliminated smallpox in Europe and North America, but it still raged in more than thirty undeveloped countries, with more than 20 million smallpox cases each year and more than 2 million deaths.

In 1967 an all-out campaign to wipe out smallpox completely was launched by the World Health Organization. Over the next ten years, in an effort that cost a total of $330 million, seven hundred physicians, nurses, scientists, and other personnel from WHO joined about two hundred thousand health workers in the infected countries to fight the disease. Traveling from village to village, they searched out smallpox cases, isolated the victims, and vaccinated everyone who had been in contact with the disease. The world's last natural case of smallpox occurred in October 1977. In May 1980, the WHO formally announced that smallpox had been completely eradicated.[3] Now scientists are hoping to use the experience gained in the successful fight against smallpox to eradicate polio.

Polio Eradication

The last naturally occurring polio case in the Western Hemisphere was reported in 1991 in Peru. Not a single case was reported for the next three years, and in 1994, polio was officially declared eradicated in the Western Hemisphere. Unfortunately, polio is still endemic in other parts of the world, particularly in three major areas: South Asia (India, Pakistan, Afghanistan), West Africa (mainly Nigeria), and Central Africa (mainly the Democratic Republic of the Congo, and a recent outbreak in Angola).[4] As long as polio still exists somewhere in the world, even if only in one or two areas, this disease will continue to be a threat. Therefore, total worldwide eradication is essential.

In 1988, WHO launched a massive campaign in the fight against polio. Its goal was to eradicate polio from the world by the end of the year 2000. At that time, approximately thirty-five thousand polio cases were reported worldwide. In 1999, the number of reported cases of paralytic polio was reduced to about seven thousand. (Not all cases are reported, however, especially in developing countries where resources are limited. WHO experts estimated that the annual number of cases as of the end of 1999 was no more than twenty thousand.)[5] Although scientists have made tremendous progress since 1988, polio eradication by the end of 2000 was not an entirely realistic goal. Many experts believe that total eradication is close, but it may not be achieved until 2005.[6]

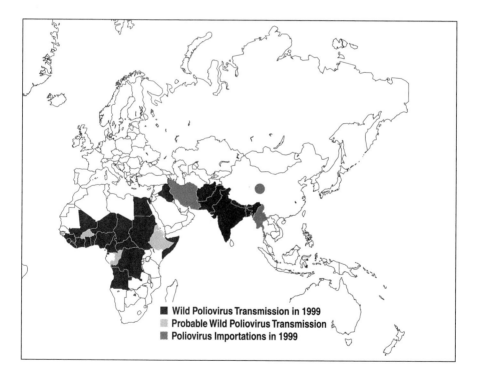

Countries with known or probable wild poliovirus transmission, as of March, 13, 2000. Polio has been eradicated in the Western Hemisphere.

In order to achieve global eradication, it would be necessary to protect every single child in the world against the virus. Fortunately, not every child would actually have to be vaccinated. Attenuated viruses in the oral vaccine are transmitted to people who come in close contact with the vaccines, and once a large enough fraction of the population was protected, the herd effect would make it difficult for the virus to reach susceptible hosts. Even so, the WHO goal would require a lot of work and a lot of money. Therefore, WHO joined forces with Rotary International, the United Nations International Children's Emergency Fund (UNICEF), the United States Centers for Disease Control and Prevention, and the governments of Australia, Britain, Canada, Denmark, Italy, Japan, Norway, Sweden, and the United States.[7]

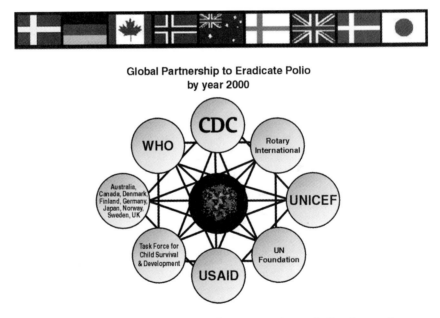

Global Partnership to Eradicate Polio by year 2000

The logo for the Global Partnership to Eradicate Polio shows the participating bodies.

Polio eradication depends on four main strategies:

1. High routine immunization coverage with the oral polio vaccine, involving at least three doses per person.
2. National Immunization Days (NIDs), on which millions of children under five would be vaccinated in a single day.
3. Effective surveillance for wild polio cases.
4. Door-to-door immunization, known as "mopping up" campaigns.[8]

In recent years the effort has been enormous. In 1996, 400 million children—almost two thirds of the world's population of children under the age of five—were vaccinated against polio. On a single day in January, 1997, 127 million children were vaccinated in India.[9] On National Immunization Day in January 2000, doses of vaccine were carried to remote regions across the country by elephants, camels, and military helicopters.[10] India, which has more polio cases than any other country, has now reached 90 percent immunization coverage.[11]

Until recently, polio was endemic in the Western Pacific region, which includes Cambodia, China, Malaysia, Papua New Guinea, the Philippines, and Vietnam, reporting thousands of cases each year. As a result of National Immunization Days, during which more than 100 million children were vaccinated within only two days, polio cases were quickly reduced to zero in 1998. China reported its last polio case in 1994. In March 1997, the last polio case of the entire Western Pacific region was reported in a one-year-old girl in Cambodia. Polio is now considered to be eradicated in the Western Pacific region.[12]

The World Health Organization has estimated that it will cost about $800 million each year to eradicate polio.[13] But the economic benefits will be much greater if eradication is achieved. Eventually, worldwide immunization may no longer

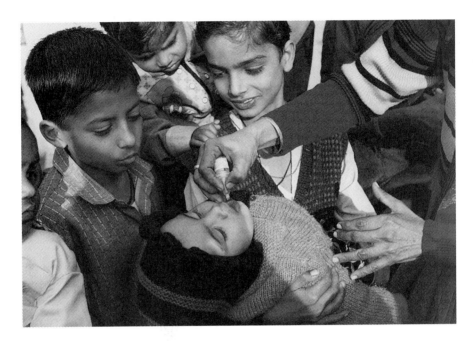

A young girl is given a dose of the oral polio vaccine in the streets of New Delhi, India. On one single day in January 1997, 127 million children were vaccinated in India.

be necessary, just like smallpox. That would translate into a savings of more than $1.5 billion each year, considering the costs for immunizations and the treatment and rehabilitation of polio victims.[14] The money saved could be directed toward other health services.

Giving a Helping Hand

Eradicating polio would be a huge relief for future generations all over the world. But how can modern science help people who already have had polio and are living with its crippling effects? Scientists have developed some amazing devices to help people

Should Polio Vaccinations Be Stopped After Eradication?

Scientists at WHO use smallpox as a model in the fight against polio. Unfortunately, the two diseases do not have the same biological basis. The smallpox vaccine contains a harmless relative of the virus that causes cowpox. Thus, the vaccine was not made from a wild virus causing the more serious disease, and, therefore, could not mutate back into an infectious form and cause an outbreak.

The oral polio vaccine, however, is made from a wild virus, and does have the potential to revert back to a virulent form. This virus can remain in the environment, in drinking water, and in the bodies of people whose immune systems are damaged. Therefore, if routine vaccination is stopped after eradication, unprotected people could still get paralytic polio from the mutated live virus persisting in the environment. The reality of this danger was emphasized by an outbreak of 19 cases of paralytic polio that occurred in 2000 in the Dominican Republic—an area where wild polio had been eradicated nearly ten years before. Medical researchers traced the outbreak to mutated OPV.[15]

Scientists are not certain how to solve this problem. Some experts, however, suggest that vaccination should continue until IPV can be distributed worldwide to reduce the risk of vaccine-associated paralytic polio.[16]

actually move their paralyzed limbs. In 1997, the Food and Drug Administration (FDA) approved a revolutionary device called the Freehand, designed to help paralyzed limbs move by activating the muscles through electrical stimulation. This device can make it possible for a quadriplegic to write a letter, drink a cup of coffee, or even to paint.

The Freehand device is surgically implanted into the person's chest much like a pacemaker, and electrodes are attached to the muscles in the arms and forearms. The device sends electric signals through the electrodes, which causes the hand to open and close. It works much like the way your brain sends signals to get your muscles to move. An external transmitter is placed outside the skin over the location of the Freehand device. The external transmitter activates the simulator by quick shoulder movements, which are picked up by a shoulder position sensor. The Freehand has been implanted into more than one hundred sixty people, who can now move body parts that have not moved in years. But health experts warn that Freehand is not for all people with paralysis. Its effectiveness depends on the individual situation.[17]

Scientists are now taking this technology even further. People with paralysis can use their own thoughts to move their muscles.

Jim Jatich, who has been paralyzed for twenty-three years, can now open and close his hand just by thinking about it. He wears a cap covered with electronic sensors that pick up his brain waves and send them to a computer through multicolored wires. The computer converts the signals from the brain waves into a kind of "on-off signal." It sends that signal to a device implanted into Jim's chest, which opens and closes his hand when he thinks "open" and "closed." These technological advances can bring a lot of hope for people who had long dreamed of writing a note, combing their own hair, or brushing their teeth.[18]

A Cure for Paralysis?

Football fans who watched the year 2000 Super Bowl on TV saw a commercial that was literally too good to be true. The commercial, made to advertise Nuveen Investments, showed a crowded auditorium in which researchers who cured spinal cord injuries were being honored. Actor Christopher Reeve, who had been paralyzed in a riding accident in 1995, got up from a chair and walked up to the stage to stand among the people who had benefited from the research.

After the game, doctors and organizations such as the National Spinal Cord Injury Association were flooded with phone calls from people who were paralyzed, or their parents and relatives, asking where they could go to get the treatment that had apparently cured Reeve. Unfortunately, the cure had not yet happened. The ad was intended to stimulate support for investment in medical research by depicting how success *might* look in the future. The commercial's images were partly simulated on computers. Criticized for raising false hopes, Reeve responded that he is optimistic that the event in the commercial is "something that can actually happen."[19]

In fact, researchers studying ways to prevent and cure paralysis have made a great deal of progress recently, suggesting that Reeve's hopes may be realistic. Until the late 1990s, scientists were convinced that if nerve cells (neurons) in the brain and spinal cord were damaged, they could not regenerate, or grow back, and no new ones were formed after infancy. As more was learned about the nervous system, however, it was discovered that by changing the conditions in the body, this kind of regeneration could be made to take place.

Each body cell is bathed in a fluid that contains a diverse mixture of chemicals, from simple salts to proteins and other complex

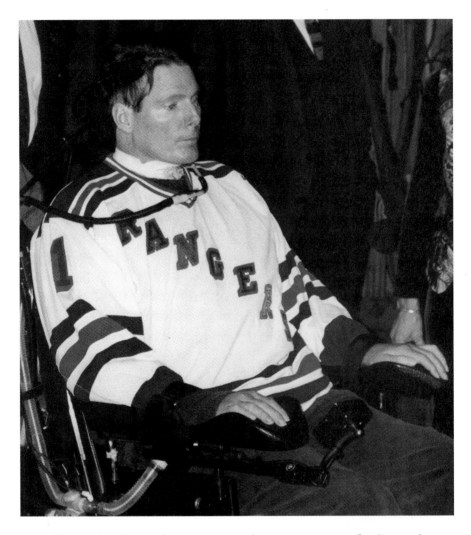

Christopher Reeve plays an active role in trying to get funding and legislative support for research into curing and preventing paralysis. In this photo taken January 8, 1999, Reeve attends a hockey event featuring the New York Rangers to benefit the Christopher Reeve Foundation and other charities.

biochemicals. Some are always present; others are produced in response to an event such as cell damage due to an injury or illness. When a nerve cell is injured, connections linking it to other nerve cells are broken. The damaged nerve cell attempts to regenerate, or regrow, its missing parts and reestablish the connections. The sensory and motor nerves in the peripheral nervous system (the nerves outside the brain and spinal cord) can do this fairly well, stimulated by body chemicals called nerve growth factors. In the central nervous system (the brain and spinal cord), however, there are also various inhibitory chemicals, which prevent regrowth.

After fifteen years of work, a Swiss group headed by researcher Martin Schwab announced in early 2000 that they had isolated a key growth-inhibiting protein. They had also created an antibody that blocks its effects. They named the protein "Nogo," because nerve cell regeneration in the central nervous system will not take place (go) when it is present. When the researchers gave the antibody against Nogo for two weeks to experimental rats whose spinal cords had been partially cut, the spinal nerve cells regrew. The rats were no longer paralyzed; they could grab food pellets and climb ropes, just as they were able to do before the injury.[20]

Meanwhile, researchers at King's College in London announced around the same time that they had succeeded in getting sensory nerve cells to reestablish their connections with a cut spinal cord in experiments on rats. They accomplished this miracle by introducing two nerve growth factors into the rats' cerebrospinal fluid. Matt Ramer, the lead researcher, commented, "In principle we have shown it is possible for sensory neurons to regenerate. That can hopefully be applied throughout the nervous system in other neurons like motor neurons, or neurons from the brain down to the spinal cord, and from there out to the muscles."[21]

Another promising approach to restoring function to paralyzed muscles is the use of cell transplants. Some researchers have reported some improvement in damaged muscle function when they took supporting cells from nearby peripheral nerves, which secrete nerve growth factors, and transplanted the cells into the cut spinal cords of rats. In another study, rat cells in culture were genetically engineered to produce a growth factor. The modified cells were then transplanted into animals with cut spinal cords, and the treated animals regained their ability to walk.[22]

It is hoped that treatments such as these may someday help to overcome paralysis, whether it is caused by a spinal cord injury or by a disease such as polio.

Controversial Research

Researchers have not been progressing as fast as they might on another promising approach to the treatment of paralysis. Experiments have shown that in mammals and other higher animals, the ability for regeneration decreases with age. Early embryos can regenerate virtually any type of cell. In fact, if cells in a very early embryo, known as stem cells, are separated, each one has the potential to produce all the tissues and organs needed for a fully independent individual. Studies on animals such as rats and cats with cut or damaged nerves have demonstrated that when stem cells taken from embryos are transplanted into the site of the damage, the cells can grow, in spite of the naturally produced inhibitory chemicals. Then these cells can restore the broken connections to motor nerves.[23]

Medical researchers are excited by the potential of work with stem cells, since they might be used to cure not only paralysis but also some ailments involving damage to the brain such as Alzheimer's and Parkinson's diseases.

However, anti-abortion activists have spoken out strongly against conducting such stem cell research on humans, because in obtaining the stem cells, the embryos are destroyed. In 1996, a ban was imposed on government funding of research in the United States involving human embryos. This ban was imposed even though embryonic cells were available from spontaneous abortions (as opposed to voluntary abortions). In addition, embryos left over after *in vitro* fertilization would provide an ample supply. (Not only could the cells themselves be used, but they can be grown and duplicated in cultures, so that huge amounts of stem cells could be obtained from a few embryonic cells.)

In an essay in *Time* magazine, Christopher Reeve pleaded for the ban on research involving human embryos to be lifted. "While we prolong the stem-cell debate, millions continue to suffer," he pointed out. "It is time to harness the power of government and go forward."[24]

In August 2000, the National Institutes of Health issued new rules permitting researchers who receive government funding to work with human embryonic stem cells, as long as the government-paid researchers themselves are not the ones who extract the cells from embryos. Stem cells would be provided by commercial firms from frozen embryos slated for destruction at fertility clinics because their owners no longer wanted them.

Commenting on the new guidelines, President Clinton stated, "I think we cannot walk away from the potential to save lives, to help people literally get up and walk, to do all kinds of things we could never have imagined, as long as we meet rigorous, ethical standards."[25]

Q & A

Q. Are polio vaccinations safe?

A. It depends on what kind. Killed injectable polio vaccine cannot cause paralytic polio. But the oral vaccine contains live virus. This virus is specially weakened so that it cannot normally cause paralysis or other serious symptoms. But in a very small number of cases, the vaccine virus can mutate and become able to cause paralytic polio.

Q. That sounds dangerous! So, why do doctors use the oral vaccine?

A. The oral vaccine has some advantages. It's a lot easier to take than an injection, it's cheaper, and it can spread protection against polio even to people who have not been vaccinated. The more people in a community who are protected, the less chance that a poliovirus could infect anyone and start an epidemic. But now that there is so little danger from polio in most of the world, doctors are changing their procedures. Now they give the first two vaccination doses with killed injectable vaccine. Then, when the child already has some protection, the third and fourth doses can be given with the live oral vaccine. United States health officials have recommended that all four doses should be of the killed vaccine type except under special circumstances. Eventually, when there is no longer any polio anywhere in the world, people may not need to get vaccinated against it. (That is what happened with smallpox.)

Q. They say there hasn't been any polio in the United States for years. So, why did I have to get polio vaccinations?

A. As long as there is polio anywhere in the world, a traveler to one of the areas where it is common could pick it up and bring it back to the United States. Then you would be in danger if you were not protected.

Q. Why do people make such a big deal about Franklin D. Roosevelt having polio? What did not being able to walk have to do with being able to be a good president?

A. You're reflecting the attitudes of your generation. Most people now realize that people with disabilities are no different from anyone else. But in Roosevelt's time, most people thought that disabilities were something to be ashamed of, something to hide. In their minds disability meant inability—they assumed that if Roosevelt could not walk, he therefore could not be a strong leader. That is why he always tried to give the impression that he could stand and walk, and the press cooperated in the cover-up.

Q. My grandfather had polio back in the early 1950s. He says his legs were paralyzed for awhile, and he worked very hard to get his strength back. But in the last year or two he's been having problems with his legs again. They tire easily and hurt a lot, and now he has to use a cane to walk. What's happening?

A. It sounds like your grandfather has post-polio syndrome. The nerves that took over to help him move his legs and walk again when he was a kid have been overworked since then. Now they are getting worn out and can no longer send signals to all the muscles.

Q. I babysit for a two-year-old girl, and her parents told me she just received a dose of the oral polio vaccine. I hear that vaccine contains a live virus. So, does that mean I can catch polio from her and get paralyzed?

A. It is not very likely, but there is a very small possibility. Make sure to wash your hands very carefully after you change her diapers. Her feces might be carrying infectious poliovirus.

Polio Timeline

1500 B.C.—An engraving on an ancient Egyptian stone depicted a priest with one withered leg, supporting himself with a staff. This was probably a person with polio.

1789—English physician Michael Underwood described the crippling effects of polio and suggested the use of braces to help children walk.

1840—German orthopedist Jacob von Heine wrote the first clear medical description of polio.

1843—Jacob von Heine used the name *infantile paralysis* to describe a condition that often affects children and can cause paralysis.

1870—Jean-Martin Charcot discovered that nerve cells in the anterior horn of the spinal cord, which control muscle movements, were damaged in a paralytic polio patient.

1887—The first polio epidemic occurred in Stockholm, Sweden, affecting 44 people. Pediatrician Karl Oskar Medin described four types of paralysis and some characteristics of the fever.

1894—The first United States polio epidemic occurred in Rutland, Vermont, affecting 132 people.

1905—Observing patients in a polio epidemic that affected more than one thousand people, Swedish pediatrician Ivar Wickman pointed out that paralytic cases were only a small fraction of the total, and people with mild cases helped to spread the disease.

1908—Austrian scientists Karl Landsteiner and Erwin Popper discovered that a virus was causing infantile paralysis.

1916—Polio struck 29,000 people in the United States, killing 6,000 of them.

1921—Franklin Delano Roosevelt contracted polio.

1929—Philip Drinker developed the "iron lung."

1940s—Australian nurse Sister Elizabeth Kenny revolutionized polio treatment in the United States. Her methods included applying hot packs to muscles and stretching exercises.

1947—The term *infantile paralysis* became outdated. Health experts decided to use the term *poliomyelitis*, which was shortened to "polio" in common usage.

1948—Harvard researchers John Enders, Thomas Weller, and Frederick Robbins discovered how to grow the poliovirus in a tissue culture using a solution made from monkey kidney tissue.

1949—Scientists discovered that there are three different kinds of polioviruses.

1952—Polio epidemics reached their peak at 57,879 reported polio cases.

1955—Jonas Salk's inactivated polio vaccine (IPV) was licensed for marketing.

1960—Albert Sabin's oral polio vaccine (OPV) was licensed for marketing.

1979—The United States reported its last case of wild polio.

1988—The World Health Organization launched a campaign to eradicate polio from the world by the end of the year 2000.

1991—The last wild polio case in the Western Hemisphere was reported.

1997—The Centers for Disease Control and Prevention recommended that the polio vaccination schedule change from four doses of OPV to two doses of IPV plus two doses of OPV.

1998—Worldwide polio cases dropped to 6,227 from 35,000 in 1988.

2000—The CDC recommended that children receive IPV rather than OPV for all four doses.

Glossary

anterior horn—An area in the spinal cord containing nerve cells that control muscle movements.

anterior horn cells—Motor neurons that send messages to control the muscles of the arms, legs, trunk, diaphragm, abdomen, and pelvis.

antibodies—Proteins produced naturally to protect the body from outside germs or other "invaders." They are produced to bind specifically to chemicals or organisms foreign to the body, such as surface chemicals on an invading virus.

atrophy—The wasting away of muscle tissue from disuse.

attenuated—Weakened.

autopsy—A physical examination after death.

cerebrospinal fluid (CSF)—A clear fluid that flows through a space that surrounds the brain and spinal cord.

cuirass respirator—A portable respirator consisting of an airtight fiberglass shell that fits over the patient's body from neck to abdomen. It is connected to an alternating-pressure pump by a hose.

diaphragm—A dome-shaped sheet of muscle that separates the chest cavity from the abdominal cavity.

endemic—Present in local populations.

eradicate—To remove or destroy completely.

Guillain-Barré syndrome—A condition that results in muscle weakness and sometimes paralysis; may be confused with polio.

herd effect—Protection of all members of a community from a disease as a result of enough of the members having been immunized against it.

immune system—Various defenses produced by the body, including white blood cells and interferon, that protect it against invading microbes.

incubation period—The time between contracting an infection and the appearance of symptoms.

infantile paralysis—An early name used to describe polio.

inflammation—Swelling, pain, heat, and redness in the tissues around a site of infection.

inoculate—To vaccinate.

interferon—A protein released by virus-infected cells that protects other cells from infection.

iron lung—A huge "coffin-shaped" metal box that uses a vacuum to pump oxygen to people whose lungs have stopped working.

larynx—The voice box.

lumbar puncture—*See* spinal tap.

meningitis—An infection of the meninges, the membranes covering the brain and spinal cord.

mutate—To change.

neurons—Nerve cells.

nonparalytic poliomyelitis—A mild form of the polio infection that does not involve paralysis.

oral vaccine—Vaccine given through the mouth.

paralysis—Loss of the ability to move.

paralytic polio—A polio infection that involves paralysis.

pathologist—One who interprets and diagnoses the changes caused by disease in tissues and body fluids.

pharynx—The throat.

poliomyelitis—The full name for polio, an infectious disease of the motor neurons in the brain and spinal cord, which may result in muscle weakness and possibly paralysis.

post-polio syndrome—The reappearance of polio-like symptoms 25 to 30 years after an original polio infection.

regeneration—Regrowth, restoration of a lost or damaged body part.

spinal tap—The collection of a sample of cerebrospinal fluid (CSF) taken with a hollow needle inserted in the gap between two vertebrae; also called *lumbar puncture.*

stem cells—Primitive cells that have the potential to develop into any cells or tissues in the body.

trachea—The windpipe.

vaccine—A preparation containing an inactivated or weakened virus or bacterium or portions of it, used to stimulate the body's production of antibodies against the germ.

vaccine-associated paralytic polio (VAPP)—A polio infection associated with the oral polio vaccine.

virologist—A scientist who specializes in the study of viruses.

virulent—Potent or poisonous.

white blood cells—Jelly-like blood cells that can move through tissues and are an important part of the body's defenses against disease.

wild polio—A case of the disease caused by poliovirus circulating in the environment.

For More Information

Centers for Disease Control Public Inquiries
1600 Clifton Road, N.E.
Atlanta, GA 30333
(404) 639-3286

Christopher Reeve Paralysis Foundation
500 Morris Avenue
Springfield, NJ 07081
(800) 225-0292

International Polio Network
4207 Lindell Boulevard, #110
St. Louis, MO 63108-2915
(314) 534-0475

Kent Waldrep National Paralysis Foundation
16415 Addison Road, Suite 550
Addison, TX 75001
(877) SCI-CURE
e-mail: kwnpf@kwnpf.org

March of Dimes Birth Defects Foundation, National Office
1275 Mamaroneck Avenue
White Plains, NY 10605
(888) MODIMES (663-4637)

The National Foundation for Infectious Diseases
4733 Bethesda Avenue, Suite 750
Bethesda, MD 20814
(301) 656-0003

National Institute of Allergy and Infectious Disease, NIH
9000 Rockville Pike, Building 31
Bethesda, MD 20892

NeuroControl Corporation
1945 East 97 Street
Cleveland, OH 44106-4720
(888) 333-4719
e-mail: skrebs@remote-ability.com

Polio Connection of America
P. O. Box 182
Howard Beach, NY 11414
(718) 835-5536

Polio Society
P. O. Box 106273
Washington, DC 20016
(308) 798-8180

Polio Survivors Association
12720 La Reina Avenue
Downey, CA 90242
(310) 862-4508

World Health Organization
200 Avenue Appia
1211 Geneva 27
Switzerland

Chapter Notes

Chapter 1. A Devastating Disease

1. Kathryn Black, *In the Shadow of Polio: A Personal and Social History* (Reading, Mass.: Addison-Wesley Publishing Co., 1996), pp. 24–25.

2. Tony Gould, *A Summer Plague: Polio and Its Survivors* (New Haven, Conn.: Yale University Press, 1995), pp. 32–33; Nina Gilden Seavey, Jane S. Smith, and Paul Wagner, *A Paralyzing Fear: The Triumph Over Polio in America* (New York: TV Books, L.L.C., 1998), pp. 45–50.

3. Thomas M. Daniel and Frederick C. Robbins, eds., *Polio* (Rochester, N.Y.: University of Rochester Press, 1997), p. 10.

Chapter 2. What Is Polio?

1. Nina Gilden Seavey, Jane S. Smith, and Paul Wagner, *A Paralyzing Fear: The Triumph Over Polio in America* (New York: TV Books, L.L.C., 1998), pp. 245–251.

2. Ibid., pp. 119–133.

3. Kathryn Black, *In the Shadow of Polio: A Personal and Social History* (Reading, Mass.: Addison-Wesley Publishing Co., 1996), pp. 15–16.

4. Marinos C. Dalakas, Harry Bartfelt, and Leonard T. Kurland, "Polio Redux," *The Sciences,* July/August 1995, p. 33.

5. Wayne Biddle, *A Field Guide to Germs* (New York: Henry Holt & Co., 1995), p. 113.

6. "Global Status of Polio Eradication," World Health Organization, <http://www.polioeradication.org/global_status.html> (March 9, 2001).

7. Thomas M. Daniel and Fredrick C. Robbins, eds., *Polio* (Rochester, N.Y.: University of Rochester Press, 1997), p. 9.

8. Black, p. 39.

9. Dalakas, et al., pp. 32–33; Healthanswers.com, "Poliomyelitis," <http://www.healthanswers.com/adam/top/view .asp?filename=001402.htm> (May 12, 1999); Louis M. Bell, Mary Lou Manning, Jane Brooks, and Marion Steinmann, *Guide to Common Childhood Infections* (New York: Macmillan, 1998), pp. 212–213.

10. Black, pp. 15–16

11. Ibid., p. 258.

12. Dalakas, et al., p. 33.

13. Gazette International Networking Institute (GINI), "Frequently Asked Questions about Post-Polio Syndrome," <http://www.post-polio.org/task/faq.html> (February 16, 2000).

14. Ibid.

Chapter 3. Polio in History

1. Thomas M. Daniel and Frederick C. Robbins, eds., *Polio* (Rochester, N.Y.: University of Rochester Press, 1997), p. 5; Kathryn Black, *In the Shadow of Polio: A Personal and Social History* (Reading, Mass.: Addison-Wesley Publishing Co., 1996), p. 23.

2. Tony Gould, *A Summer Plague: Polio and its Survivors* (New Haven, Conn.: Yale University Press, 1995), p. 10.

3. Ibid.

4. Ibid., p. 11; *Encyclopaedia Britannica* (Chicago, Ill.: Encyclopaedia Britannica, 1973), vol. 18, p. 155; Michael B. A. Oldstone, *Viruses, Plagues, and History* (New York: Oxford University Press, 1998), p. 94.

5. Daniel and Robbins, p. 7.

6. Naomi Rogers, *Dirt and Disease: Polio Before FDR* (New Brunswick, N.J.: Rutgers University Press, 1996), p. 141.

7. Kathryn Black, *In the Shadow of Polio: A Personal and Social History* (Reading, Mass.: Addision-Wesley Publishing Co., 1996), p. 24.

8. Daniel and Robbins, p. 8.

9. Black, pp. 26–27.

10. Ibid., p. 24.

11. Ibid., pp. 72–75.

12. Daniel and Robbins, pp. 10–11.

13. Black, p. 28.

14. Louis M. Bell, Mary Lou Manning, Jane Brooks, and Marion Steinmann, *Guide to Common Childhood Infections* (New York: Macmillan, 1998), p. 211.

15. Michael B. A. Oldstone, *Viruses, Plagues, and History* (New York: Oxford University Press, 1998), pp. 96–97.

16. Ibid., p. 96.

17. Daniel and Robbins, p. 11.

18. Oldstone, p. 98.

19. Daniel and Robbins, pp. 11–12.

20. Ibid., pp. 11–14.

21. Gould, pp. 66–68.

22. Nina Gilden Seavey, Jane S. Smith, and Paul Wagner. *A Paralyzing Fear: The Triumph Over Polio in America* (New York: TV Books, L.L.C, 1998), p. 167; Rogers, p. 173; Black, p. 217.

23. Seavey, et al., pp. 168–175.

24. Oldstone, p. 108.

25. Seavey, et al., pp. 164–176.

26. Peter Radetsky, *The Invisible Invaders* (Boston: Little, Brown and Company, 1991), p. 128.

27. Maggie Yax, personal communication, June 29, 2000.

28. Seavey, et al., pp. 176–177.

29. Black, p. 256.

Chapter 4. Diagnosing and Treating Polio

1. Peg Kehret, *Small Steps: The Year I Got Polio* (Morton Grove, Ill.: Albert Whitman & Company, 1996).

2. Dr. Paul G. Donohue, "Guillain-Barré causes weakness in muscles," *Newark Star-Ledger*, February 8, 2000, p. 36.

3. Louis M. Bell, Mary Lou Manning, Jane Brooks, and Marion Steinmann, *Guide to Common Childhood Infections* (New York: Macmillan, 1998), p. 213.

4. Kathryn Black, *In the Shadow of Polio: A Personal and Social History* (Reading, Mass.: Addison-Wesley Publishing Co., 1996), pp. 83–84; Thomas M. Daniel and Frederick C. Robbins, eds., *Polio* (Rochester, N.Y.: University of Rochester Press, 1997), p. 10.

5. "And They Shall Walk," <http://www.thehistorynet.com/ NationalHistoryDay/teacher/willwalk.htm> (February 21, 2000).

6. Ibid.; Peg Kehret, pp. 125-129; Australian Broadcasting Company, "Sister Elizabeth Kenny," 1998, <http://www.abc.net.au/ btn/australians/ekenny.htm> (January 27, 2000).

7. Tony Gould, *A Summer Plague: Polio and Its Survivors* (New Haven, Conn.: Yale University Press, 1995), p. 92.

8. Richard Hill, "Each Saving Breath," 1997, <http://members .xoom.com/_XMCM/jprestwich/jprest1.html> (November 30, 2000).

9. John Prestwich, "40 Years a Layabout!" 1996, <http:// members.xoom.com/_XMCM/jprestwich/40years.html> (November 30, 2000).

10. Hill, "Each Saving Breath"; Maggie Prestwich, personal communication, March 23, 2000.

11. Liz Ford, "Freedom after 44 Years," *Watford Free Observer*, September 28, 1999, p. 1; Maggie Prestwich, personal communication, November 1, 2000.

12. Hill, "Each Saving Breath."

Chapter 5. Preventing Polio

1. Daniel Jack Chasan, "The Polio Paradox," *Science*, April 1986, p. 37.

2. Ibid., pp. 37–38.

3. Centers for Disease Control, "Questions and Answers on Simian Virus 40 (SV40) and Polio Vaccine," March, 1999, <http:// www.cdc.gov/nip/vacsafe/vaccinesafety/sideeffects/SV40.htm>;

Doctor's Guide, "No Link Found Between Contaminated Polio Vaccine and Cancer," January 27, 1998, <http://www.pslgroup .com/dg/52BC2.htm>; Doctor's Guide, "Polio Vaccine Poses No Risk According to Canadian Vaccine Expert," February 4, 1997, <http://www.pslgroup.com/dg/19D66.htm>; "SV40 virus and polio vaccine," <http://www.who.int/gpv-safety/hottop/sv40.htm> (February 16, 2000).

4. "Parents' Group Supports Decision for Use of Safer Polio Vaccines for Children," December 9, 1998, <http://www.ipav.org/ vappnews.html>.

5. "Parents' Group Applauds Decision to Switch to Safer Injectible Polio Vaccine for Children," June 17, 1999, <http://www.ipav.org/vappnews.html>.

6. "Notice to Readers: Recommendations of the Advisory Committee on Immunization Practices: Revised Recommendations for Routine Poliomyelitis Vaccination," *Morbidity and Mortality Weekly Report*, July 16, 1999, p. 590.

7. Karen Hsu, "Pediatricians Urge Use of Safer Polio Virus," December 7, 1999, <http://neuroscience.about.com/...on/ neuroscience/library/pr/blpr991207c.htm>.

Chapter 6. Polio and Society

1. Nina Gilden Seavey, Jane S. Smith, and Paul Wagner, *A Paralyzing Fear: The Triumph Over Polio in America* (New York: TV Books, L.L.C., 1998), p. 61.

2. Polio Survivor's Page: "President Franklin Delano Roosevelt: A Disability Hero," April 4, 1995, <http://www.eskimo .com/~dempt/ fdr.htm>.

3. "Roosevelt: The Perfect Presence," p. 3, <http://www .academic.marist.edu/1/ssp/fdr2.htm> (February 29, 2000).

4. Robert Mauro, Polio Survivor's Page: "Photographs of Franklin Delano Roosevelt," 1996, <http://www.eskimo.com/ ~dempt/ fdrpic.htm>.

5. Ibid.

6. "FDR Memorial will depict Roosevelt in wheelchair," 1998, <http://www.nandonet.com/newsroom/ntn/nation/070298 .nation27_21971_noframes.html>.

7. About.com, "The Franklin Delano Roosevelt Memorial: Pt. 1–The Controversy of a Statue," <http://americanhistory. about.com/education/americanhistory/library/weekly/aa050597> (January 28, 2000).

8. Tom Rhodes, "Disabled condemn FDR to wheelchair," July 3, 1998, <http://freerepublic.com/forum/a369293.htm> (November 30, 2000).

9. "FDR Memorial will depict Roosevelt in wheelchair," 1998.

10. Seavey, et al., p. 62.

11. U.S. News Online, April 7, 1997, "The spin on Clinton's knee," <http://www.usnews.com/usnews/issue/970407/7peop.htm>.

12. U.S. Dept. of Justice "Americans with Disabilities Act" ADA home page, <http://www.usdoj.gov/crt/ada/adahom1.htm> (February 29, 2000).

13. Seavey, et al., p. 234.

14. Jim Vertuno, "Disabled golfer teaches others," *The Courier-News* (Bridgewater, N.J.), July 9, 2000, p. A-4.

15. Maggie Jackson, "Disabled get help, but more is needed," *The Courier-News* (Bridgewater, N.J.), March 15, 1999, p. A-8.

16. John Langone, "When Friends and Family Fill Most of a Patient's Medical Needs," *The New York Times*, October 14, 2000, p. F8.

17. Anna Mulrine, "Barbie joins the real world," *U.S. News & World Report*," June 2, 1997, p. 11; Christine Sokoloski, "New doll adds diversity to Barbie's world," *The Courier-News* (Bridgewater, N.J.), June 3, 1997, p. A-1.

18. John Prestwich, "40 Years a Layabout!" 1996, <http:// members.xoom.com/_XMCM/jprestwich/40years.html>; Maggie Prestwich, personal communications, May 20 and August 14, 2000.

19. Maggie Prestwich, "Who Cares?" 1991, <http://members .nbci.com/_XMCM/prestwich/who_cares.html>.

Chapter 7. Polio and the Future

1. *The World Book Encyclopedia* (Chicago, Ill.: World Book, 1988), vol. 17, p. 216; Wayne Biddle, *A Field Guide to Germs* (New York: Henry Holt & Co., 1995), p. 132.

2. Peter Radetsky. *The Invisible Invaders* (Boston: Little, Brown, & Co., 1991), pp. 31–35.

3. *The World Book Encyclopedia* (Chicago, Ill.: World Book, 1988), vol. 17, p. 216.

4. Press Release WHO/21, "Polio Outbreak in Central Africa," April 9, 1999, <http://www.who.int/inf-pr-1999/en/pr99-21.html>.

5. The Jordan Report 2000 (Bethesda, Md.: NIAID, NIH); "Poliomyelitis," Fact Sheet No. 114 (Geneva: WHO, February 2000), p. 1.

6. Press Release WHO/55, "Pasteur Merieux Connaught Donates 50 Million Doses of Polio Vaccine for War-Torn Countries," October 11, 1999, <http://www.who.int/inf-pr-1999/en/pr99-55.html>.

7. The Associated Press, "Without immunization, disease spreads," *The Courier-News* (Bridgewater, N.J.), January 4, 1998, p. A-7.

8. Press Release WHO/21.

9. Nina Gilden Seavey, Jane S. Smith, and Paul Wagner, *A Paralyzing Fear: The Triumph Over Polio in America* (New York: TV Books, L.L.C., 1998), p. 277.

10. Miriam Jordan, "With Elephants, Loudspeakers and Violet Dye, India Fights Polio," *The Wall Street Journal,* March 23, 2000, pp. B1, B4.

11. The World Health Organization: Regional Office for South-East Asia, "Polio Eradication: The Final Push India, And the World Will Make It, Says WHO," August 20, 1999, <http://www.whosea.org/tcg/lucknow/lucknow_details_1.html>.

12. "WHO Announces Landmark in Polio Eradication," March 19, 1999, <http://www.who.org.ph/whatsnew/press/1999/wppr006.htm>.

13. Seavey, et al., p. 278.

14. The Associated Press, "Without immunization, disease spreads," *The Courier-News* (Bridgewater, NJ), January 4, 1998, p. A-7.

15. "Public Health Dispatch: Outbreak of Poliomyelitis—Dominican Republic and Haiti, 2000," *MMWR*, December 8, 2000, p. 1094.

16. "When Polio Is Gone, Should We Still Vaccinate?" August 8, 1997, <http://128.59.173.136/PICO/Chapters/News897.html>.

17. Kristi Coale, "An Electronic Helping Hand," August 19, 1997, <http://www.wired.com/news/news/story/6160.html>; <http://abcnews.go.com/onair/CloserLook/wnt_000214_CL_paralysis_feature.html>; Victor D. Chase, "Mind Over Muscles," *Technology Review*, March/April 2000, <http://www.techreview.com/articles/ma00/chase.htm>; NeuroControl Corporation, "The Freehand System," <http://www.remote-ability.com/unique/freehand.htm> (March 8, 2000).

18. Jack Smith, "New Spinal Realities," February 14, 2000, <http://abcnews.go.com/onair/CloserLook/wnt_000214_CL_paralysis_feature.html>; Victor D. Chase, "Mind Over Muscles," *Technology Review*, March/April 2000, <http://www.techreview.com/articles/ma00/chase.htm>.

19. The Associated Press, Jim Fitzgerald, "Reeve TV ad fooled some," *The Courier-News* (Bridgewater, N.J.), February 2, 2000, p. A-6.

20. Jeff Barnard, "Gene ID'd in Spinal Cord Injuries," Associated Press release, January 26, 2000, <http://wire.ap.org/APnewscenter_story.html?FRONTID=SCIENCE&STORYID=AP IS727NFQO0>.

21. Emma Reid, "Spinal cord regeneration in humans one step closer to reality," January 20, 2000, Discovery Channel Canada, <www.exn.ca/html/templates/htmlpage.cfm?id20000120-57>.

22. Lydia Kibiuk, "Spinal Cord Repair," June 1997, <http://www.sfn.org/briefings/spinal_cord.html>.

23. Xiao-Zhong Liu, John W. McDonald, et al., "Transplanted embryonic stem cells survive, differentiate and promote recovery in injured rat spinal cord," *Nature Medicine*, December 1999, pp. 1410–1412.

24. Christopher Reeve, "Use the Body's 'Repair Kit'," *Time*, May 1, 2000, p. 60.

25. Nicholas Wade, "New Rules on Use of Human Embryos in Cell Research," *The New York Times*, August 24, 2000, p. A1.

Further Reading

Books

Acosta, Virginia Lee Counterman. *Polio Tragedy of 1941*. Salem, OR: First Books, 1999.

Burge, Michael C. and Don Nardo. *Vaccines: Preventing Disease*. San Diego, CA: Lucent Books, 1992.

Cohn, George C., ed. *The Wordsworth Encyclopedia of Plague & Pestilence*. Collingdale, PA: DIANE Publishing Company, 2000.

Draper, Allison Stark. *Polio*. New York: Rosen Publishing Group, 2000.

Hargrove, Jim. *The Story of Jonas Salk & the Discovery of the Polio Vaccine*. Danbury, CT: Children's Press, 1990.

Naden, Corinne J. and Rose Blue. *Jonas Salk: Polio Pioneer*. Brookfield, CT: Millbrook Press, 2001.

Nourse, Alan E. *The Virus Invaders*. Danbury, CT: Franklin Watts, 1992.

Sherrow, Victoria. *Polio Epidemic: Crippling Virus Outbreak*. Berkeley Heights, NJ: Enslow Publishers, Inc., 2001.

Articles

Chasan, Daniel Jack, "The Polio Paradox," *Science*, April 1986, pp. 37–39.

Dalakas, Marinos C., Harry Bartfeld, & Leonard T. Kurland, "Polio Redux," *The Sciences*, July/August 1995, pp. 30–35.

———, "Post-Polio Syndrome," *Science & Medicine*, May/June 1999, pp. 54–63.

Zamula, Evelyn, "A New Challenge for Former Polio Patients," *FDA Consumer*, June 1991, pp. 21–25.

Internet Addresses

Gazette International Networking Institute, International Polio Network, and International Ventilator Users Network
<http://www.post-polio.org>

The Global Polio Eradication Initiative
<http://www.who.int/vaccines-polio>

Global Status of Polio Eradication
<http://www.polioeradication.org/global_status.html>

Polio Experience Network
<http://www.polionet.org>

Index

BOSTON PUBLIC LIBRARY

WITHDRAWN
No longer the property of the
Boston Public Library.
Sale of this material benefits the Library.

Codman Sq. Branch Library
690 Washington Street
Dorchester, MA 02124